AVOIDING WORK-AT-HOME SCAMS

By
William C. Pollard

I dedicate this to Ritzel, who has been supportive of all I have done for the past eleven years. She even came up with some changes that I ended up making to this book.

AVOIDING WORK-AT-HOME SCAMS

"For the time will come when men will not put up with sound doctrine. Instead, to suit their own desires, they will gather around them a great number of teachers to say what their itching ears want to hear. They will turn their ears away from the truth and turn aside to myths." *2 Timothy 4: 3-4 (NIV).*

PURPOSE OF THIS PUBLICATION

The above quote from the *New Testament* obviously is not directed at work-at-home scams. It is concerned with false teachings that plagued the early Christian church. This quote shows people were being influenced by that which sounded too good to be true. Everyone should have sound religious beliefs. As well, they should have sound financial beliefs.

Before you spend money on any work-at-home program, you must read this book. I have thoroughly researched work-at-home programs, so you don't have to research into them. You paid for my research when you bought this book. I have enjoyed the research that I have done. However, I am ever so disappointed that there are so many persons out there who show no remorse at scamming others.

I will mention here that I quote directly word for word from some sources. In such cases, I have decided the sources presented their information more clearly than I could have summarized it. However, I have recognized these sources each time I quoted from them, as they deserve full credit for what they have said. Also, I did not quote entire articles. I have provided notes so you can visit the websites themselves, if you want additional information.

First, let me present to you my qualifications for the opinions and information I am about to present to you. PPP Travel Consulting, a business we established in 2005, was run until 2013. We were registered with the Florida Department of State Division of Corporations from the beginning to the end of the company's life. We were also registered with Highlands County, Florida. Further, the company paid income tax since 2006 to the IRS for every year it existed.

PPP Travel Consulting was established to provide consulting to those needing information when they were planning travel. Interestingly, this was always our smallest source of income. Our two larger sources of income came from our residential cleaning service and our customer service consulting. For a time, we also provided contract respiratory services, as the author of this publication is a respiratory therapist. When the economy in general had a severe downturn, we eventually closed the business when we saw fewer and fewer profits. We closed on good terms, however, and only lost a bit of money the last year the company existed.

Various topics will be presented in this book. Let's list them:

- First, we will examine one of the most common work-at-home scams, processing mail from home.
- Pyramid schemes and multi-level marketing.
- Assembling products at home.
- Check cashing scams.
- Reshipping or processing money.
- Medical billing scams.
- Medical transcription scams.
- Real estate scams.
- Rebate processing.
- Survey scams.
- Mystery shopping scams.
- Internet selling scams.
- Data entry and typing scams.
- Freelance writing scams.
- Anti-scam sites.
- Phishing.
- How to determine whether a proposal is legitimate or is a scam.
- Legitimate possibilities for making money from home.

PROCESSING MAIL FROM HOME

There are always advertisements and flyers proclaiming you can make a living, if not a fantastic fortune, processing mail from home. Here are quotes from some of them:

- "**$1,400-$2,800** weekly potential! Mailing letters. Free details. Start immediately. . . ."
- "**1,000 ENVELOPES** = $5,000. Receive $5.00/envelope stuffed with our sales material. Guaranteed!"
- "**EARN AN EXCELLENT WEEKLY INCOME PROCESSING MAIL!! $3.00 FOR EACH ENVELOPE YOU PROCESS. . . .** We require a onetime completely refundable deposit of only $44.95 for the program."
- "**MAKE $1,400 TO $2,800 WEEKLY GUARANTEED! IN JUST A COUPLE OF HOURS A DAY. . . .** Just fill out the short application form below and send it in with your **$39.00 FULLY REFUNDABLE DEPOSIT. . . .**"
- "Using our program, you process our sales brochure for $5.00 each and receive **payment before you mail them. . . .** We ask only for a **one-time returnable deposit** of $25 + $5.00 S/H. . . ."

9

All of the above opportunities are scams. I'm going to tell you why in the following sections.

COMMON MAIL SCAMS

STUFFING ENVELOPES

This is at times is the most common mail processing scam. There are several variations on this scam. The most common is one where you get information saying you can make high rates of pay for stuffing envelopes with flyers or brochures. As in the examples above, the sales pitches make income claims that are fantastic.

Here is how this scam works. You see an ad in a tabloid making unbelievable claims about income and directing you to call a number for information or write to an address or enter a website.

Next, you get a response in the form of a flyer. In it you are told a high level of income is possible. The examples above are typical. The flyer may claim such high rates are being paid, because a client is far behind schedule on an advertising project and desperately needs help.

The response always requires a refundable deposit to get you started. It is always said this is to cover administrative costs for those who want to start work, but never follow through. You are assured once you stuff a certain number of envelopes, that your deposit will be returned. The price is never really high, almost always in the $30.00 to $50.00 range. The money can be paid by check, money order, credit card or sometimes cash.

Most people who decide to do this send their money to the mailing company and wait. They almost never hear from the company again. If they do, they are sent another list of companies to contact for envelope stuffing work. If they contact these companies, either they never get a response or are told these companies do not pay people to stuff envelopes. In other words, someone just randomly pulled a company address out of a website, telephone book, etc., and sent the address to the people they scammed.

The mailing company may have a telephone number listed in their literature. However, if you try to call the number you always find it is either not a working number, is never answered or is answered by answering machine. In the latter case, no one ever returns your telephone call.

Some of these companies even have realistic-looking websites. About fifteen years ago, I looked into something to make a little extra money at home. I rejected most of the ads in the tabloids. One, however, had as its contact information a website, rather than listing a post office box or telephone number.

I looked at the website, which had a number of options in it. It asked for a $30.00 refundable deposit along with the online application to use its services. I was not as knowledgeable about scams as I am now. I sent a check for $30.00 and never heard from the company after waiting two months. I then investigated further. I tried to call the toll-free number, but no one ever answered. The company listed an address in New York City. I contacted the New York Attorney General and they had several consumer complaints about the company. I contacted the telephone company and they said this number was being operated from New Jersey. Eventually, the number was disconnected, although the website remained in place.

Back then theft identity was not as sophisticated as it is now. However, this venture started me on a quest to find more information about various scams that exist.

Responding to any of these ads can result in unexpected and even unwanted consequences. These scammers may sell your address to another scam artist or scam artists. You may then receive mail from other scammers with similar or even totally different scams to entice you.

You may even have your credit information stolen. This is especially true if you pay by check or credit card. The last thing anyone needs these days is to have their credit or bank information hijacked and then find himself owing for things he never authorized or having money stolen from his bank accounts or cash advanced against his credit cards.

The UK also has envelope stuffing scams. An online article in the website of the UK newspaper *The Guardian* and posted on February 1, 2005, ("Scams," written by Sandra Haurant) says:

The advert in the show window says you could earn a fortune working from home stuffing envelopes. You could do with the extra cash, and you've always been good at stuffing envelopes, so you call the number. They ask for a registration fee, which seems strange for an envelope stuffing job, but you pay up, and then you receive a copy of the same advert which you are supposed to stick in the window of another shop. You feel used. All they wanted was your registration fee.

CHAIN LETTER REQUIRING YOU TO BUY A MAILING LIST

Another approach I have seen has you mailing loads of envelopes that you stuff with a flyer encouraging the recipients to mail even more envelopes. This is a scam that could get you into trouble with the Postal Service. I ran into this one, because someone I knew sent it to me. Because I knew the victim, I was able see up front how this worked. My friend said he wondered whether this project was legal, but got involved with it anyway.

This scam worked as follows. My friend was sent an envelope with a flyer. The flyer made fantastic claims about people who made great amounts of money following the instructions given in it. At the end of the instructions were ten names and addresses of persons to whom he was to send $2.00. These were people higher up on the list. The recipient was told that he could join in the wealth by buying a mailing list of 100 names with addresses printed on labels. My friend was to purchase them from a company listed in the flyer. The cost was $29.95 and $4.00 shipping and handling.

He sent away for the labels and said they arrived in a couple of weeks. So far, so good. He was to change the flyer by taking the first name off the list and placing his name and address at the bottom. Next, he was to make 100 copies of the altered flyer and stuff them in standard business-size envelopes.

The original letter told him to send $2.00 to each of the ten persons on the list. The idea was really a pyramid scheme. If each of the 100 persons receiving the letter sent money to the names on it and sent it to 100 more people, there would then be 10,000 persons involved. If each of these persons sent out 100 letters, then 1,000,000 people would be involved. Pretty soon the whole world would be involved and you would be rich with all the $2.00 installments coming to you.

And to make you really motivated to send your letters, a paragraph in the offer told of dire consequences suffered by those who received it and did not send any copies out, such as death, loss of loved ones, loss of jobs, etc. Most chain letters, incidentally, promise disaster if the chain is broken.

My friend sent out his 100 copies and $2.00 to each of the ten people on the list. He never heard anything about this again. He never received any payments from anyone. This is typical for most pyramid projects; at some point they just fade away.

HOW TO DETECT MAIL PROCESSING SCAMS

There are a number of ways to detect mail processing scams. In fact, I could find no projects for processing mail from home that were not scams. The following sections tell you how to detect scams and the ideas presented to detecting any kind of scam, not just mail scams.

CHECK WITH YOUR STATE ATTORNEY GENERAL

The various state attorney general offices are involved with scams and consumer protection. These are invaluable resources. All have web sites with information about scams and companies against whom complaints have been filed. I received a great deal of information from some of them and from there I was able to direct further questions to individuals in these offices. Feel free to access a website from a state attorney general anywhere in the country. While each site is set up for the benefit of its state's residents, the information posted is free to be accessed by anyone anywhere in the world.

One link that provides contact information for the attorney general websites of the fifty states, the District of Columbia and five U.S. territories is the National Association of Attorneys General, at http://www.naag.org/naag/attorneys-general/whos-my-ag.php . This site provides website addresses for the individual state and territory attorneys general. An attorney general is responsible for consumer protection, which includes keeping tabs on scams.

Now, let us look at a few of the websites from across the country. This will give you an idea about what help and information is available.

Florida's website presence, http://myfloridalegal.com/consumer , provides many answers concerning consumer protection issues and fraudulent schemes.

The Kansas website, www.ksag.org/home/ , provides a similar service and lists various tips regarding consumer protection.

Maine's site, www.maine.gov/ag/ , has a good consumer protection link in it. The Maine website also devotes a large web page to providing information about various fraudulent schemes.

The website for Alaska, www.law.state.ak.us/ , has a consumer protection link containing several web pages concerning consumer fraud.

All websites provide telephone numbers where specific complaints can be made or detailed information can be gotten. You may ask whether the state consumer protection office has information about specific companies not appearing in their websites. Also, you can just ask who you reach whether a specific ad's claims seem right.

I contacted both the Kansas and the Florida attorney general offices by telephone about several issues. I asked the Florida office about specific companies. I was told it is impossible to keep up with work-at-home scams, as people running them will open a post office box, run it a short while, close it down and then open a new box in another location under a new name. Sometimes they get caught, but more often they just move around as their old business name is trashed because of consumer complaints. Keep in mind even when a scam runs out of websites that they can close, rename and open at will, there is a physical location somewhere that can be found.

The Kansas attorney general's office provided an additional piece of information. I was told over the telephone it is possible there somewhere is an envelope stuffing scheme that is legitimate and provides what it promises. However, the contact person on the phone told me their office had never heard of anything but scams concerning mailing schemes.

Sometimes attorney general offices know information they are not at liberty to discuss. Sometimes state legal restraints prevent the disclosure of information. Sometimes ongoing investigations prevent disclosure and complaints legally cannot be disclosed. I asked the Arizona Attorney General's office about information on a particular company and they were unable to help me. They provided me with a summary of their disclosure policy, as follows:

> The Attorney General's office cannot say if a business is or is not legitimate. . . .
>
> Complaints and investigations that we may have are confidential and cannot be disclosed to the general public by Arizona law. Our office can only disclose information on any lawsuits that may have been filed by the Attorney General.

OTHER CONSUMER PROTECTION AGENCIES

Other agencies exist that provide information about companies about which you have questions. These include chambers of commerce, the Better Business Bureau and the various states' departments of revenue. Also, a number of other sites are discussed, as are a few other tips.

CHAMBERS OF COMMERCE

Local chambers of commerce can tell you whether a company within their jurisdiction is a member. If they are, this is good. If they are not, it by no means says they are bad companies. We had a business for several years that was not a member of the local chamber of commerce, as we thought, for the level of income we made, the fee to join was steep. If we made a full-time income from this business, we would have definitely joined.

Also, chambers of commerce may tell you what they know about a particular company. If they have heard bad things, it is possible someone from their office will tell that. They may not, however, if they really have no solid evidence of misbehavior. They do not want to become involved in a slander or libel charge.

Look up chambers of commerce in telephone books or on the internet by searching for a particular city or county and then searching for its chamber of commerce.

BETTER BUSINESS BUREAU

The Better Business Bureau is another source of information about a company's reputation. Its home page is www.bbb.org . A number of options are available for you. First, you may search for a business reliability report. If the BBB has information concerning a company, you will find it thru the search. Sometimes, businesses do not have a reliability report. The lack of a report does not mean a company is bad. It simply means a company does not have a history of any type with the BBB. A report with many complaints and with a number of unresolved complaints should be enough to steer you away from the company in question.

I will soon tell you what the BBB says about its rating process. When one reads the standards the BBB sets, he would think he could rely on a positive report about the business. In reality, the only time you can use a BBB report with confidence is when a report on a business is negative. A negative report always means a business has at least a few unresolved customer service issues.

I found through my research that a good report does not mean a business has a good reputation. I have looked at the reports the BBB gave for a number of businesses. I purposely picked a number of businesses that have had a number of legitimate complaints voiced about them in other reputable forums. In only a few cases did the BBB issue an unsatisfactory report. In all other cases these businesses were issued satisfactory reports and in one case an excellent report was issued.

First, I will relate what I found about the reports of two healthcare businesses, both of which will remain anonymous here. Neither provides customer service I would rate highly. One type of rating the BBB uses runs from A+ for excellent to B for above average to C for satisfactory to D for poor to F, the latter grade meaning a company should be avoided at all costs.

One facility indeed had a "D" rating. This was based on several items. One was a complaint brought to the BBB. This business did not respond to the complaint brought to the BBB. Also, the BBB requested information from this business and, again, this business ignored the request. When the BBB brings complaints to a business, the business must make a good-faith attempt to resolve and report its actions back to the BBB. When the BBB requests background information from a business, again, it reflects badly in the BBB's rating when a business does not respond.

The second healthcare operation had no complaints brought against it through the BBB. Furthermore, this operation provided the BBB with the background information it requested. This business had an "A" rating.

I looked into the BBB's assessment of one of the big multi-level marketing (MLM) companies. It came out with a satisfactory rating and has been a BBB accredited business for years, although, again, this company has had serious valid criticisms thrown at it.

Finally, I looked into a couple of the real estate "experts" who have made sensational claims. They say you can buy property with no or very little money down. Both have had serious and valid criticisms lodged against their claims. One has operated for years. One had a satisfactory rating and the other had an unsatisfactory rating.

Not many business experts criticize the BBB. However, I found one criticism of it several years ago by Undress4Success (http://undress4success.com). This website provides much information about work-at-home scams and about legitimate ways to work from home. Undress4Success said, "Unfortunately, the [BBB] won't be much help because the worst [MLM scams] frequently change their name and address. So no one's really watching out for your interests. And the fact is some of the [BBB's] practices should be reported to the Even Better Business Bureau (but that's a topic we'll have to remember for another post)."

I would really like to see that post once it is written. A news story written by the Associated Press and appearing nationwide in the January 4, 2009, issues of many newspapers adds credence to what Undress4Success says.

The story points out that the BBB's budget is paid by its members:

> Critics say there's a conflict of interest in the organization's operations because its funding comes primarily from dues paid by member companies. Some also have expressed concern that the bureau may treat members more favorably than nonmembers when complaints are filed.

> Daylian Cain, an assistant professor at the Yale School of Management, said conflict of interest is a problem for any organization that serves two groups.

> "It doesn't mean that [bureau officials] are engaged in criminal activity, but it's very dangerous," Cain said. "The problem is (it's hard) to be totally objective when one is serving two groups and one of them is paying the bills."

In the story William P. White, CEO for the BBB of Southeast Florida and the Caribbean, explained the mission of the BBB. "'We don't represent the consumer,' White said, explaining the bureau is not a consumer advocacy group. 'We represent ethical business practices.'" ("Better Business Bureau Busier Than Ever," *Highlands Today* (Sebring, Florida), January 4, 2009, Business sec., pp. 1, 3.)

This fully explains that the BBB is not directly protecting the consumer, although that is a major purpose of upholding ethical business practices. However, after more criticism in 2010, the BBB said it would make sure it would rate nonmember companies exactly the same way its member companies were rated.

A 2013 story in the *New York Times* documented the BBB's changed policy concerning differences in ratings of member versus nonmember companies:

> In 2011, David Segal, who writes The Haggler column for *The New York Times*, did a series looking at customers' complaints about the bureau.
>
> Since then, the bureau has made some changes. It used to give an A plus only to accredited businesses, [Katherine] Hutt [a BBB spokesperson] said. That is no longer true.
>
> "That was misinterpreted as pay for play," she said. "Accredited and unaccredited are now judged

exactly the same." (Alina Tegund, "Sizing Up the Better Business Bureau, and Its Rivals on the Internet," *New York Times* online, November 15, 2013, at http://www.nytimes.com/2013/11/16/your-money/sizing-up-the-better-business-bureau-and-its-rivals.html?_r=0 .)

Now let us look at what the BBB uses to come up with company ratings.

A company may be recommended for accreditation with the BBB. There are a number of standards that must be met for a company to have BBB accreditation. Members must keep good reputations to remain accredited. Companies that are not accredited are not necessarily bad. Some good companies have not sought accreditation. Part of the reason is financial. To become accredited costs a fee. For small businesses, more fees are not always something they can afford.

Let's look at what the BBB's accreditation standards are.

First, the company must have been in operation at least six months. The business must sign the Accredited Business Application and pay dues and fees set by the BBB. Background information about the business and its owners/backers must be provided.

The business must fulfill all licensing and bonding requirements set by the jurisdictions in which it operates, such as cities, counties, states and federal agencies. The license numbers must be provided to the BBB.

Good customer service is required. The company must respond to any complaints brought to the local BBB branch's attention. The company must make a good faith effort to resolve all complaints. Complaint prevention policies must exist that meet the BBB's approval.

The business must not have an unsatisfactory report on file in the local BBB service area.

The company must comply with any decisions rendered thru BBB arbitration programs in which the company participates.

The firm must agree to self-regulation within its industry. It must also agree to abide by BBB standards on advertising and selling.

The business must be free from any governmental action concerning its market practices.

Two standards involve upholding the image of the BBB. One says the firm cannot use the BBB name or logo for promotional purposes not specifically authorized by the BBB. The second standard requires the firm to refrain from engaging in activities that adversely reflect on the BBB or its accredited businesses.

It is clearly seen from these standards, that when a business is accredited by the BBB, it would seem it can be trusted by the consumer. My research casts doubts on this.

The BBB has branches all over the U.S. and Canada. You may search the BBB website to either find a branch near you or near where a subject company is located.

Also, the BBB, in its website, provides general consumer information about detecting scams. It provides information about some of the common scams and it provides tips about differentiating scams from real opportunities.

After examining how the BBB rates companies, it seems there are several factors that skew the rating system:

- It appears that only a very few dissatisfied consumers register complaints with the BBB. Only complaints brought to the BBB are investigated by it.
- Since only a few complaints are brought to the BBB, maybe a company experiencing many consumer complaints will only concentrate on those brought to it through the BBB. It would be easy to address those few complaints and get a satisfactory rating. All the complaints never reaching the BBB could be ignored, as they would not affect the BBB rating process.
- There is a related issue to the one just stated. I have found companies that have several company names associated with them. All happen to have BBB reports on them. One or maybe more of the

companies will have at least a satisfactory rating. This company name seems to be used to show the world it is an honest enterprise. This company will do everything it can to keep its good rating. It will respond to any complaints brought to its attention by the BBB. However, if you look at some of the other company names used by the business, you find they have unsatisfactory ratings. They do little or nothing to respond to complaints brought to the BBB's attention.

- A few paragraphs above I stated that a company must stay free of problems with governmental regulatory agencies and have a clean reputation with the BBB. I am at a loss how some companies can be given satisfactory ratings or even be accredited.

In conclusion, the BBB does provide some useful information. If it gives a business a bad rating, it is wise to avoid that business. A bad rating means a company is not trustworthy. Also, the BBB provides some general consumer information concerning scams. As was said before, some bad companies are given satisfactory to excellent ratings by the BBB. After what I found, I do not trust any but unsatisfactory ratings of businesses by the BBB.

YELP

The story by Alina Tegund ("Sizing Up the Better Business Bureau, and Its Rivals on the Internet") mentioned two other services that provide information that in some ways compares to the BBB. Tegund wrote about Yelp, "Another option is Yelp, which compared to the Better Business Bureau . . ., is either sheer anarchy or refreshingly open. Anyone can look up a company on Yelp or leave a review."

Yelp is a San Francisco based service. Here is what Yelp says of itself, "Yelp is the best way to find great local businesses. People use Yelp to search for everything from the city's tastiest burger to the most renowned cardiologist. What will you uncover in your neighborhood?" (Yelp website, at http://www.yelp.com/orlando-fl-us .) As Tegund wrote, Yelp relies on customers to review and rate various businesses, using a system of one to five stars. One is the worst possible rating and five is the best possible rating. A number of sites allow customers to leave reviews and ratings, including Amazon.com and TripAdvisor. The problem is when some individuals go online, they lose all sense of tact and good manners. Some individuals get downright insulting to other reviewers.

I once quit reviewing on Amazon for a few years when a few persons went beyond disagreeing and were personally insulting. The same problem can happen with Yelp.

In one graduate research class I learned something called content analysis. One part of content analysis involves examining a source based on how reasonable the statements made in the text seem. Take notice of how a person critical of a company makes his or her complaint. If he or she states that this company in question is the worst company in the world when talking about a fairly minor complaint, take the complaint with a grain of salt. While there could be some truth to the complaint, an exaggerated description of what happened probably is not true.

ANGIE'S LIST

Tegund also mentioned Angie's List in the *New York Times* story. Angie's List puts safeguards into its review of companies by the public in an attempt to prevent the skewed reviews and ratings mentioned above. Angie's List is a reporting service that a user has to join, so it is a bit different than Yelp. Angie's List says of its process:

> **Our data is certified.** Before they're posted, all reviews are checked in order to guard against providers and companies that try to report on their own companies or their competitors. This process was reviewed and approved during a 2012 audit by BPA Worldwide. (Angie's List website, at http://www.angieslist.com/how-it-works.htm/?gclid=CJ2opozZp8YCFdgXgQodPakAAg&CID=HowItWorksSitelink&s_kwcid=AL!3718!3!82581841121!e!!g!!angies%20list'&ef_id=VQe6QAAABKrL2wOR:20150624062511:s .)

BPA Worldwide is a company devoted to auditing such things as the reliability of reviews of services and businesses by the general public. (BPA website, at www.bpaww.com/ .)

STATE DEPARTMENTS OF REVENUE OR DEPARTMENTS OF STATE

The various state departments of revenue or departments of state may be contacted concerning a company's status. Most states have at least some information concerning legitimate companies that operate within their borders. In Florida, for instance, companies are supposed to register their names with the Department of State Division of Corporations. The consumer may also find financial information or consumer alerts on companies in some of the states. Just search on the internet for the appropriate agency.

RIPOFF REPORT

One source that claims to provide information about frauds and scams is Ripoff Report (www.ripoffreport.com). It does expose some scams. It has an index, so it is not difficult to find complaints filed against businesses.

However, due to its nature, it also sometimes trashes the names of legitimate companies. The reason for this is Ripoff Report posts any complaints anyone has about a business. These reports are only screened to delete personal information and curse words. Otherwise, little in the way of screening is done to find whether a complaint is legitimate. In Ripoff Report's defense, accused companies are allowed to post their responses to complaints.

I found one company with which I have done work over the years listed there. I know it has high standards. I found two posted complaints about it that would lead anyone to believe the business is just a scam.

I would not say to avoid Ripoff Report. Useful information about companies can be found there. I would, however, avoid making a judgment solely on complaints reported there. See whether these reports are consistent with information from other sources.

Inaccurate posts on companies has resulted in a few legal actions against those posting complaints and Ripoff Report for posting them. In May 2013, Ripoff Report started offering a new service called "Ripoff Report Verified" that allowed companies fourteen days to resolve complaints before they were posted, for an $89.95 a month company membership fee.

For further information about Ripoff Report, please see the article "Ripoff Report" in Wikipedia (http://en.wikipedia.org/wiki/). The Wikipedia article provides details about a number of shortfalls and changes for the better with Ripoff Report.

OTHER SOURCES OF INFORMATION ABOUT SCAMS

About.com – This website has a page (http://jobsearch.about.com/cs/workathomehelp/a/homesc am.htm) that provides some tips about evaluating the legitimacy of work-at-home ads. It also lists a number of work-at-home jobs to always avoid. This website is actually a component of the New York Times Company, which publishes *The New York Times*.

The United States Postal Service (USPS) – The USPS website has a page (http://about.usps.com/publications/pub300a/pub300a_tech_018.htm) promoting a publication that provides some tips when considering work-at-home opportunities. The USPS also allows you to order a free work-at-home scam DVD. The DVD, *Work@Home Scams: They Just Don't Pay!*, is mainly focused on the reshipping scam, to be discussed later in this book. It does say a bit about envelope stuffing scams and product assembly scams. This DVD shows what can happen when unwary individuals fall for scams. It also provides tips for recognizing scams.

The Federal Trade Commission (FTC) – The FTC has a section in its website (http://www.consumer.ftc.gov/articles/0175-work-home-businesses) concerning work-at-home opportunities and scams. This section contains a wealth of information concerning scams. In the FTC home page (www.ftc.gov) you can search for companies to see whether the FTC has investigated them.

National Consumers League Fraud Center – This organization's website has a page (www.fraud.org/tips/internet/workathome.htm) that also provides tips to evaluate work-at-home opportunities. There are two organizations with similar names. To differentiate, this is the organization located in Washington, DC.

Home with the Kids – This organization is geared toward stay-at-home moms and dads who would like to make a bit of part-time income from home. It has a newsletter for which you can subscribe for free. Its website also has many web pages devoted to examining work-at-home offers and finding the scams amongst them. For this information, please see www.homewiththekids.com/scams/ .

Home-Based Working Moms – This is another organization that offers tips on revealing scams to stay-at-home parents wanting to make a part-time income from home. It has a web page on scams (www.hbwm.com). One tip I would not recommend following says, "Try to use your credit card instead of cash if you invest in a business opportunity. That way if you do want a refund, it may be easier to dispute the charges with your credit card company."

If you are at all worried an opportunity is not above board, never use a credit card. If the offer is a scam, the scammer may be into stealing credit card information.

If you desire further information from Home-Based Working Moms, you may pay a membership fee to belong to it. Currently, the dues for new members are $69.00 for a one-year membership or $129.00 for a two-year membership. Renewing members receive a discount.

Undress4Success – This is a website (http://undress4success.com) associated with Kate Lister and Tom Harnish. Through their website they sell books about home business opportunities. The site has a wealth of articles about work-at-home opportunities and scams. They also post reader responses to their articles.

Computer Crime Research Center – This is a volunteer organization that has worked in the past with the Federal Bureau of Investigation (FBI) and the Merchant Risk Council to investigate crime with internet connections. This organization is international in character, with strong connections to crime researchers in Russia, the Ukraine, South Korea, Belarus and France. Their website (www.crime-research.org) says they are always looking for new volunteer researchers.

Merchant Risk Council – This organization was formed in 2002 by a handful of companies to educate online merchants to help prevent fraud. It quickly grew, with more than sixty members. The Merchant Risk Council has coordinated operations with the FBI and the Computer Crime Research Center to combat internet fraud. Its website is www.merchantriskcouncil.org .

Federal Bureau of Investigation – The FBI has investigated some work-at-home scams and has participated in raids and arrests of scammers. To get more information on what the FBI has about scams, you may visit the FBI website, www.fbi.gov .

Truston – This business provides online identity theft prevention and recovery services. Truston's website, www.mytruston.com , has a section devoted to scams. The ones mentioned are mostly not work-at-home scams, but a few of them are noted. You can subscribe to a free online newsletter or pay fees to subscribe to Truston's services.

Snopes.com – Snopes.com (www.snopes.com), owned and run by Barbara and David Mikkelson, aims to confirm or debunk widely spread urban legends. It is very reliable. For the most part, Snopes has very little information about work-at-home scams. I found, however, once in a while it has something to offer. If you hear of an offer to make money on unusual things from several sources, check out Snopes to see whether anything helpful is there.

Knowledgeable persons – See what persons knowledgeable about a particular activity say about it. If they think it is not an honest proposal they will tell you why.

Registration with governmental/business authorities – A company engaged in a legitimate business activity will probably be registered with at least a couple of regulatory authorities or professional business groups. Ask these questions:

- Is this business registered with an appropriate state authority? Check with the state department of revenue where the business is located to see what requirements must be met for regulation. A state may require registration of a business name or a sales tax license.

- Is the business registered with a local authority? Many cities or counties require some sort of registration for a business, such as an operating license or license to collect sales tax.
- What is the reputation of the business with the Better Business Bureau? If it has a checkered reputation, watch out.
- What does the local chamber of commerce know about a business? Is it a member? Local chambers may have information about a business.

Advertising from the business – Does this business advertise in such a way as to sensationalize?

- Does the advertising promote this business as a get-rich-quick scheme? If the advertising promises or suggests huge income with only a small amount of work, it is screaming "SCAM, SCAM, SCAM." One article on scams sums this concept up nicely, "If something seems too good to be true, it is." (Gladys Sherrer, "Protect Yourself From Scam Artists," *Renewed & Ready*, November 2008, p. 23.)
- DOES THE ADVERTISING MAKE USE OF ALL CAPITAL LETTERS, EXAGERATED OVERSIZE LETTERS, BOLD TYPE, OVERUSE OF COLORS OR GARSIH COLORS, MANY EXCLAMATION POINTS AT THE END OF EACH SENTENCE?!!!!!! This last sentence got your attention, didn't it? Advertising overusing these methods should be viewed with caution.

- Does the ad promote excessive urgency? If the ad says the offer is to end almost immediately or says it is a once in a lifetime offer, stay away from the product. Very, very, very few offers are such that they must be acted upon immediately or lost to the consumer forever.

Other tips to remember – These are other tips not really covered anywhere else. If you have any questions about an ad or offer make use of these.

- If the advertisement provides endorsements from other businesses, check out these endorsing businesses using the same criteria as you use in checking the business with the work-at-home offer. Check the endorsing business with the regulatory authorities, the chambers of commerce, the Better Business Bureau, etc. A firm with a bogus offer will not hesitate to provide itself with endorsements from either nonexistent firms or other firms engaged in questionable activities. If the endorsing company is known to be legitimate, contact this company concerning its endorsement. It is always possible a scammer may provide a phony endorsement from a reputable company.
- If the ad provides endorsements from professional associations, go through the steps detailed in the above point. A scammer is not above conjuring up a name for an association that is to provide an endorsement. Also, I have run across scammers who invented a couple of professional associations that had contact information. These associations were

real, but were only in existence to attempt to provide the scammer with legitimacy it did not have.

- In 1999, it could be said more scams originated in certain parts of the U.S., in particular Florida. However, today scams seem to be located everywhere in the country. This is partly because many, if not most, scams today have an internet connection. The internet allows a company to operate anywhere in the US, if not from a foreign location. Therefore, what you may have heard about scams being located in certain parts of the U.S. is no longer true. Also, many ads do not provide postal addresses as contacts anymore. They only provide email addresses, websites and telephone numbers. They may even have Facebook pages, although Facebook will shut down a page when complaints start being made.

These three figures show examples of phony certifications scams will use in attempts to convince you they have legitimate standing.

HOW TO REALLY MAKE MONEY PROCESSING MAIL

Can you really make money processing mail? The answer is yes, you can. However, most people are not prepared to invest the necessary time and money to do what is needed to start such an enterprise. Anyway, the business they would end up with could not remain a work-at-home business, because it would be too large. You would probably have to buy a franchise and none allow you to run your business from home. Let us take a look at some legitimate mail processing businesses: Mail Boxes Etc./the UPS Store, Goin' Postal, Pak Mail, Postal Connections, PostNet. You could also start up a mail service. We will look at that option last.

MAIL BOXES ETC./THE UPS STORE

Mail Boxes Etc. and the UPS Store are one and the same, since UPS bought Mail Boxes Etc. in 2001. This is a good opportunity if you have the resources to buy a franchise. A franchise must be run from a storefront location, not out of a home or garage. You must have serious capital available to you to get into this company. The company requires liquid capital available from the applicant of more than $60,000. If accepted for a franchise, the franchise fee for a newcomer to the company is $29,950. Furthermore, startup costs to open a new shop range from $139,673 to $353,580, according to company estimates and depending on whether you want to open up in a rural or what is called a "traditional" location.

For more information see www.mbe.com/wfo/index.html .

GOIN' POSTAL

This is another mail service franchise. Again, you must run this franchise from a storefront. The cost to get into this franchise varies, depending on what you want the parent company to do and what you are willing to do for yourself. The franchise fee for Goin' Postal is $15,000 and you must pay $4,700 for one point of sale system (POS). You must pay an additional amount for equipment, rent, remodeling a storefront to meet your needs, etc. The total cost, if you remodel yourself, is around $48,865. If you have a contractor remodel, you may pay out an additional $40,000 or more.

If you want the company to do everything, which is the Goin' Postal turnkey option, you may pay the company as much as $139,500. There is an additional $420.00 per month royalty fee for an operating franchise. The Goin' Postal website says of this, "We know what it costs us to support an established franchisee each month, and we have set our $420.00 monthly royalty slightly above this amount . . . ." For further details, see the Goin' Postal website, www.goinpostal.com/goin_postal_shipping_store_franchise_info.php .

PAK MAIL

Pak Mail is another mail company from which you can buy a franchise. The minimum financial requirements to qualify for a franchise are that you have $50,000 cash or liquid assets and that your total net worth is at least $150,000. The initial investment to open a Pak Mail franchise ranges from $133,900 to $180,200. The Pak Mail website is www.pakmail.com/franchise .

POSTNET

PostNet is another that sells franchises. The cost to open a franchise with PostNet ranges from $175,000 to $197,600. PostNet's website is www.postnetfranchise.com/franchiseprogram/ . This website has only telephone contact information. To get more information, you may want to call the toll-free number listed in the website: (800) 843-7171.

POSTAL CONNECTIONS

Finally, there is Postal Connections. The cost to open a Postal Connections franchise ranges from $131,000 to $153,950. The Postal Connections website is www.postalconnections.com/storefranchise.asp .

STARTING YOUR OWN INDEPENDENT MAIL SERVICE

It is possible to start your own mail service. However, if you do, it probably will take up much time and hard work. First, you would need to find one or more companies that would contract with you to process mail for them. Possibly companies would contract with someone to handle special advertising mailings, so they would not need to do it in house. You would need to make telephone calls and visits to companies you think could be interested.

You could open a small storefront mail service. Locally, we had someone open first one shop and then two. They closed the second shop later, but the first one seems to be thriving just as well as the local Goin' Postal down the same street.

INCOME AND SOCIAL SECURITY TAXES ON PROFITS

Finally, you must be aware of income taxes, should you buy into a franchise or start any type of business for yourself. I have used Turbotax Home & Business edition for my personal and business income tax submissions. I have found Turbotax to be highly reliable. It guides you through everything you need and if you have questions, you can get answers (although you may need to dig a bit to find the right questions to ask).

You may want to use a professional accountant, if your taxes are complicated. Keep in mind, you may claim any legitimate business expenses, such as postage, office supplies, mileage, etc. Also, if you make a certain amount of profit (in 2009 it was more than $400.00) you will need to pay a social security tax on the profits. This is no big deal, as any accountant can help you. Turbotax actually fills in the paperwork for you. This allows you to pay social security tax with your federal income tax submission.

OTHER SCAMS

"Food gained by fraud tastes sweet to a man, but he ends up with a mouth full of gravel." *Proverbs 20:17 (NIV).*

Mailing and envelope scams are by no means the only types of work-at-home scams. At least fourteen other scams come to mind. Let's take a look at each.

PYRAMID SCHEMES AND MULTI-LEVEL MARKETING

Pyramid schemes and multi-level marketing schemes are quite tricky to figure out sometimes. The reason is multi-level marketing plans are sometimes legitimate business opportunities in whole or in part. All I have seen depend somewhat on a pyramid structure. This will be discussed after we first look at what "pyramid schemes" and "multi-level-marketing" (MLM) plans are. I have looked into good definitions of both and I found good descriptions of both in Wikipedia.

Incidentally, some people scoff at Wikipedia, since anyone can write articles for it and most articles may be edited by anyone. However, research into the reliability of Wikipedia has found its information to be more reliable than that from the big-name general reference encyclopedias. I speculate that is because most writers of articles for Wikipedia are experts in their fields and are very conscientious. I myself have written a number of Wikipedia articles.

First, the term "pyramid scheme" must be defined. A good definition of this term can be found in the article "Pyramid scheme" from Wikipedia. It is described as "a non-sustainable business model that involves the exchange of money primarily for enrolling other people into the scheme, without any product or service being delivered."

True pyramid schemes are illegal in the US, the UK, Canada, Australia, New Zealand and many other countries.

Wikipedia further says of pyramid schemes:

> There are other commercial models using cross-selling such as multi-level marketing (MLM) . . . which are legal and sustainable, although there is a significant grey area in many cases. Most pyramid schemes take advantage of confusion between genuine businesses and complicated but convincing moneymaking scams. The essential idea behind each scam is that the individual makes only one payment, but is promised to somehow receive exponential benefits from other people as a reward. A common example might be an offer that, for a fee, allows the victim to sell the same offer to other people, or receive bonuses through other people they

refer. Each sale includes a fee to the original seller.

. . . [T]he flaw is that there is no end benefit; the money simply travels up the chain, and only the originator (or at best a very few) wins . . . . [T]he people in the worst situation are the ones at the bottom of the pyramid; those who subscribed to the plan, but were not able to recruit any followers themselves.

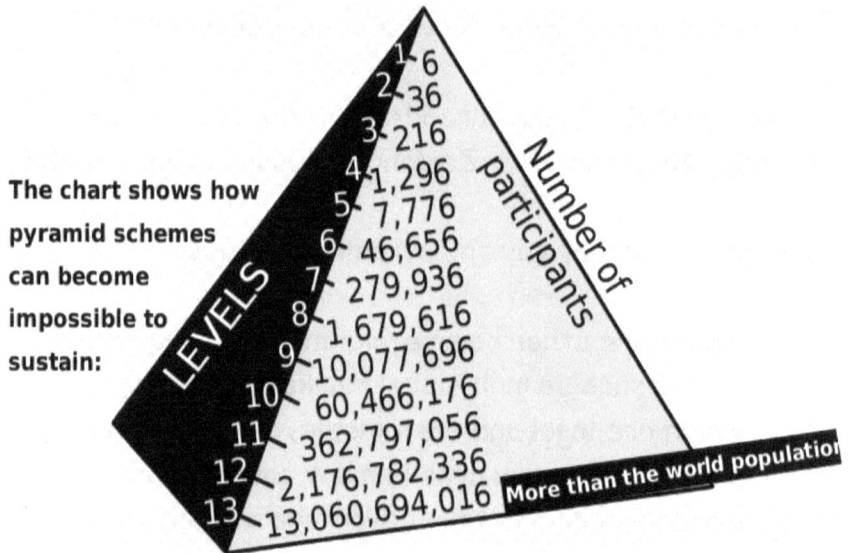

The chart shows how pyramid schemes can become impossible to sustain:

LEVELS

Number of participants

1 - 6
2 - 36
3 - 216
4 - 1,296
5 - 7,776
6 - 46,656
7 - 279,936
8 - 1,679,616
9 - 10,077,696
10 - 60,466,176
11 - 362,797,056
12 - 2,176,782,336
13 - 13,060,694,016 More than the world population

Diagram of pyramid scheme, if it works perfectly and if everyone joining it recruits an equal number of downline participants. From "Pyramid scheme," http://en.wikipedia.org/wiki/ .

MLM plans sometimes are similar to pyramid schemes. However, MLM plans do involve the sale of products, so the plans are usually legal. However, due to the way many MLM plans are conducted, the originators of the plans are not completely (or sometimes not at all) honest about the potentials for profit from their plans.

The article "Multi-level marketing" from Wikipedia defines MLM as such, "Multi-level marketing (MLM), also known as Network Marketing, is a business-distribution model that allows a parent company to market its products directly to consumers by means of relationship referrals and direct selling."

This article further says of MLM:

> Independent, unsalaried salespeople . . ., referred to as distributors (or associates, independent business owners, dealers, franchise owners, sales consultants, . . . etc.), represent the parent company and are awarded a commission based upon the volume of product sold through each of their independent businesses (organizations).
>
> Independent distributors develop their organizations by either building an active customer base . . . or by recruiting a *downline* of independent distributors who also build a customer base . . . . Additionally, distributors can also earn a profit by retailing products they

purchased from the parent company at wholesale price.

The USPS had a bulletin in its website that discussed MLM plans. Unfortunately, the page containing the bulletin no longer exists. I still have a hard copy of the bulletin. Since I cannot say it better myself, I will quote whole paragraphs from the USPS bulletin:

> Some entrepreneurs have built successful companies on the concept because the main focus of their activities is their product and product sales.
>
> However, there are many multi-level distributorship schemes that are nothing more than sophisticated chain letters. They operate as a "pyramid," claiming participants can earn lots of money by concentrating most, if not all, of their efforts on recruiting distributors rather than selling a product.
>
> The success of a pyramid distributorship . . . depends on continuously getting additional people to join the pyramid. However, there is a practical limit to how many distributors can be found and how many product units they can sell or use . . . .
>
> To protect yourself against falling victim to a multi-level marketing scheme, note whether the basis of the promotion is the sale of a product

at the retail level, as opposed to an emphasis on recruiting more and more distributors to help you increase your income.

There is no easy way to wealth. A multi-level marketing scheme is no exception . . . .

The Federal Trade Commission (FTC) shares similar ideas about MLM plans in a November 1996 memo in its website, www.ftc.gov . The FTC memo adds a few more tips about evaluating MLM opportunities. Excerpts from the memo are here quoted:

Beware of plans that ask new distributors to purchase expensive inventory . . . .

Be cautious of plans that claim you will make money through continued growth of your "downline" - - the commissions of sales made by new distributors you recruit - - rather through sales of products you make yourself . . . .

Beware of plans that claim to sell miracle products or promise enormous earnings . . . .

Beware of . . . "decoy" references paid by a plan's promoter to describe their fictional success in earning money through the plan . . . .

Don't pay or sign any contracts in an "opportunity meeting" or any other high-pressure situation. Insist on taking your time . . . . Talk it over with your spouse, a knowledgeable friend, and accountant or lawyer . . . .

Check with your local BBB and state Attorney General about any plan you're considering - - especially when the claims about the product or your potential earnings seem too good to be true.

The large MLM companies use another feature described in the "Multi-level marketing" Wikipedia article. This is the stair step breakaway plan. Wikipedia describes this as such:

This type of plan is characterized as having representatives who are responsible for both personal and group sales volumes. Volume is created by recruiting and by retailing product. Various discounts or rebates may be paid to group leaders and a group leader can be any representative with one or more downline recruits. Once predefined personal and/or group volumes are achieved, a representative moves up a step. This continues until the representative . . . "breaks away" from their upline. From that point on, the new group is no longer considered part of his . . . upline group . . . . Stairstep Breakaway plans are not level based.

This article lists various criticisms of MLM companies. It says, "Some MLM programs feature intense motivational programs, which can be hard to distinguish from cult propaganda. So-called corporate cults are businesses whose techniques to gain associate commitment and loyalty are in some ways similar to those used by traditional cults. Amway associates are sometimes cited as an example of such devotion."

Three large MLM companies are Amway, Shaklee and Herbalife. The websites for all say you can make a lot of money with their system if you are willing work hard. All put quite a bit of emphasis on recruiting people to join the plan under you. Herbalife's website does give some statistics about its distributor incomes. In its website, www.herbalife.com , it says, "Over 25% of Distributors reach the rank of Supervisor and above . . . . The annual gross compensation paid by Herbalife to Active Leaders [starting with the Supervisor] during 2006 averaged approximately $5,100."

I will not go into any detail about the claims Amway, Herbalife or Shaklee make to potential distributors, as I would have to go a recruiting meeting to get that information. I will let you decide whether you want to go to one of their meetings. I did go to a number of Amway recruiting meetings in the 1980s and 1990s and the main emphasis was on recruiting people to be under you. I also attended a Herbalife meeting about 2005 and the main emphasis again was on recruiting people to be under you once you joined. I was involved in Amway twice, ending any association with the company in 1997. Things may be different now, but I will say I found working through Amway back then to be a nonexistent way for me to make any meaningful income. The year I made any profit I only made about $200 and I worked hard to earn that.

Some individuals make an income selling Herbalife products part-time and maybe some persons sell full-time. Herbalife does offer help to individuals who want to primarily sell products, rather than recruit new associates. We have a neighbor who decided to sell Herbalife products. She opened a small retail shop in an office building and sells from that. I have never heard her try to recruit anyone to sell Herbalife. Like almost any home business, however, being successful takes much effort.

I will refer you to the Undress4Success website. A posting by one of the Undress4Success directors, Kate Lister, is entitled "Mary Kay, Amway And Other Scams." Here is how the posting starts:

> We hate to be cynics, but we've found an awful lot of work-at-home deals that turn out [to] be scams—legal perhaps, but scams none the less. If . . . you *need* to earn a living—Mary Kay, Amway and others like them are not the answer.

> [MLM] . . . sounds like a great way to make money and meet new people. But over and over they've been shown to only make money for a few people at the top of the pyramid. Their ads sound great, but when you read the fine print, there's a fee to join, inventory to buy, or lots of other out-of-pocket expenses—which, of course, is how the company or person promoting the "opportunity" really makes money.

Unfortunately, the people who run these scams often target people who desperately want a better income, but can least afford to gamble . . . . They sound great on the surface, but you'll be hard-pressed to find anyone who can show you proof that it's worked for them. Oh, sure, there'll be a few people that did okay (and they'll no doubt be filling [our] comments section with screams of protest), but most people don't.

Unlike franchises, which are required to jump through all kinds of hoops, *business opportunities*, as they're called, are largely unregulated.

This posting, sure enough, did get some negative responses, mostly from persons objecting to having Mary Kay labeled as a scam. I researched into the way Mary Kay operates. I would not go so far as to label it a scam, since people can make money by selling its products to customers. I did uncover some valid criticisms, however. For further information about Mary Kay's business practices, examine the Mary Kay website (www.marykay.com). The "Mary Kay" article in Wikipedia should prove helpful; this article points out some shortcomings of Mary Kay.

Up to May 2012, a wealth of information, including a free book (*The Merchants of Deception*) could be downloaded from the site, www.amquix.info . The site still exists, but some items in it cannot be accessed anymore. The site is still active and individuals continue to add information and posts to it. This site, founded and run by Scott Larsen, has a book's worth of information about Amway and its practices. Larsen decided to start this site for several reasons. The most important was that he had joined Amway and was very disillusioned by the time he left the organization.

Second, he said he wanted to help people avoid the mistakes he made. In his website, he says, "I thought people could learn from my experience and save the time and money I spent learning about the very real and poor business and economic aspects of Amway."

Third, he thought someone should remain out there to criticize Amway's tactics. In his site he says a couple of critics' sites closed, because of the legal costs of fighting Amway subpoenas in a particular legal case involving Amway.

Fourth, Larson said in 2010 in his site:

> The more visitor feedback I got from people really burned [by the] business, the more important it was to tell their stories. My site has so much contributed by site visitors I can hardly take credit for the site. All I've done is basically take information and documents sent to me and created a clearing-house for all of it.

Scott Larsen claimed in 2010 that he had made the Amway management very angry and possibly for a short time he stopped working on this site after this. I contacted him and found Larsen was very careful to make sure what his site said about Amway could be verified, so that he could not have a legal action filed against him. We traded emails back and forth for a while and found our past experiences with Amway were similar. We also found we had both been Eagle Boy Scouts.

There exists a site that defends Amway, Amwaywiki.com. It has a section in which the most notable critics of Amway are attacked. The part of the site devoted to the critics is www.amwaywiki.com/Critics . Some of the critics probably have little ammunition, as the site claims. However, every single critic is attacked as being basically ignorant about Amway and that is not the case with all the critics.

Now to give Amway what it is legally due. The Wikipedia article "Amway" looks at why Amway is legal. Sources cited there say Amway is a "legal pyramid scheme." The Federal Trade Commission in 1979 said, quoting Wikipedia, "Amway does not qualify as a pyramid scheme because distributors were not paid to recruit people and had to sell products to get bonus checks. . . . The FTC did, however, find Amway 'guilty of . . . making exaggerated income claims.'"

Amway claims things have changed and some news sources tend to back that up. However, finding news about Amway in the United States does not show much. Most news stories in the latest five years concern sporting events that have Amway as a sponsor or in stadiums that have Amway in their names. Amway and Herbalife do have very good products and a few individuals have found ways to market the products and ignore the multilevel marketing aspects of these organizations.

Home with the Kids also says much about MLM scams in its website. I would like to post here the whole article, but if you really want to see everything, refer to www.homewiththekids.com/scams/mlm.php .

Here are the most important parts of the article:

> The first thing you need to know is that you cannot be paid just for recruiting members. This is a sign of a pyramid scheme, and such schemes collapse when there are no new members being recruited, . . . assuming they don't get shut down first. You don't want to get caught in the legal tangle of an illegal pyramid being shut down! And if you're one of the last recruited, you just lose your money. . . .
>
> What about their income claims or claims made about their products? Do they seem reasonable? Remember, if you join an opportunity, you are responsible for any claims you make in your advertising, even if the materials were supplied to you by the company. Do your homework and know what is reasonable. Make sure all claims can be substantiated.

MonaVie is another MLM program. As do the others, MonaVie puts emphasis on recruiting distributors. Its website, http://jeunessetransition.com/ (formerly www.monavie.com), does provide detailed information about incomes. The lowest three levels, comprising 91% of all distributors, are listed as making the following average weekly incomes:

- Distributor average   44% of distributors   weekly $32
- Star average   36% of distributors   weekly $41
- Star 500 average   11% of distributors   weekly $82

MonaVie markets nutritional products.

If you do decide to take a look at these and any other MLM organizations, what I am saying about MLM organizations should help you make a decision. Let's summarize what has been said, since I have pulled tips from a variety of sources:

- See whether the plan is really selling something. If not, it is a pyramid scheme, which is illegal.
- Does the person presenting the plan tell things that even the literature they give you does not mention? I have found persons who present their plans who will say anything at all to get you to join, even if what they say contradicts the written handouts.
- Is there any or very little emphasis on you developing a base of retail customers? Does the plan or presenter emphasize recruiting new people under you to expand your business? If the answer

to the first question is "no" and the answer to the second is "yes," proceed with caution.

- Does the plan or presenter tell you if only you work hard or follow the plan, that you can become wealthy? Similarly, does the plan or presenter promise or strongly hint you will make enormous earnings? Remember what the USPS said, "There is no easy way to wealth."
- Does the plan ask its new distributors to purchase expensive inventory or require a costly entrance fee? Be wary if the answer is "yes."
- This is similar to a point made above. Does the plan claim most or almost all the money to be made with it is through commissions of sales made by distributors you recruit rather than through sales you make yourself? If the answer is "yes," be careful.
- Totally ignore testimonials made by the presenter or the literature about how someone has made a fortune joining an MLM plan. These could be either true or false; you just have no way to verify testimonials, unless you can find information about them on the internet. Unscrupulous persons will fabricate tales to lure you into their plans.
- Never sign up for a plan at the first meeting where the plan is presented. Always take the information away with you and discuss it with someone else, preferably someone with a good business background and not involved with an MLM plan.
- Check the plan with your local chamber of commerce and your (or any other) state attorney general, as these groups may have consumer complaints and

alerts about MLM plans. However, I found the national headquarters of MLM plans many times are rated at least satisfactorily by the BBB. The national headquarters may have little relationship to distributors out in the field who could make fictitious claims about the plans. As I said before, I have found the BBB to only be a reliable source of information when it rates a company badly. Too many bad companies are slipping through its scrutiny with satisfactory or even excellent ratings.

- Make sure you know whether the plan is a stair step breakaway plan. If it is, remember this plan is not level based. A distributor in such a plan would do better to hope his downline distributors do not advance to the point where they break away from him. If they do, he no longer will get commissions from these or the persons under the breakaway distributor.

- Does the MLM group put pressure on you to join right away and want you to start recruiting people immediately? If a plan is a good one, there is no need to make immediate decisions about joining it. Your decision can wait a few days.

- Sometimes worrisome features to a plan do not surface until after you join the plan. Once you join, is there pressure to set up meetings or go to meetings several times a week or almost every day of the week? If so, you probably would be best to drop out of the plan. After all, you need time to rest and relax when you are away from work.

- Does the opportunity require you to spend money to engage in it before you are completely informed as to how the particular plan operates?
- Some MLM plans or other opportunities advertise themselves as opportunities as seen on TV, as seen in the *New York Times*, as seen in *USA Today*, etc. Maybe they have been seen there and, then again, maybe they have not. You can always search online to see whether these claims are real.
- Similarly, a scam is not above touting seals of approval from legitimate organizations, such as chambers of commerce, the BBB, etc. A number of scams have as well touted impressive-looking seals of approval from organizations that sound wonderful, but that in reality do not exist and never have existed.

ASSEMBLING PRODUCTS AT HOME

A number of ads tell you that you can make extra income or even a living assembling the advertiser's products at home. I know a person who had a friend answer one of these ads. The person thought assembling knickknacks would be a good way to make some extra money at home. She answered the ad and the unassembled products were shipped to her, once she sent a refundable deposit to the company. She said she spent about 200 hours assembling these knickknacks. She then had to pay the shipping to have them sent back to the company with which she was working. The company then informed her that the products did not meet their production standards and refused to pay her for her work or refund her deposit.

The Florida attorney general website (http://myfloridalegal.com) says of the product assembly scam, "In the product assembly or craft work scheme, the company often hits you up for extra costs for supplies, equipment, etc. Then, after you have performed the work and assembled 200 sewn and hand-painted dolls, the company rejects them as not meeting their quality standards. In reality, no product ever meets their quality standard because they never intended to pay anyone."

I researched into a number of work-at-home product assembly programs. I found none I would trust. One I found seemed possibly honest, but when I checked it out with a couple of consumer protection sites, I found nothing but serious complaints from persons dealing with the program. After what I found about product assembly at home, I conclude all these programs are scams, as I never found an honest one.

Undress4Success basically says the same thing about home assembly jobs:

> The concept of doing arts and crafts work at home, building little toys, electronic components, or jewelry and getting paid [for] it is appealing to many people and is something virtually anyone can do. The problem is *you* pay for the materials and shipping. Do you think Ford charges it's assembly line workers for the car parts?. . .

Finally when you send the results of your labor in they say your work isn't good enough and refuse to pay.

Home with the Kids, which we described in the above discussion about mail processing scams, concurs almost all home assembly programs are scams. It says, "Don't bother with the ads offering you the chance to assemble crafts for someone else . . . . There are very, VERY few legitimate assembly jobs out there. If there is any kind of fee, forget it!" For more on this, see the Home with the Kids website and appropriate webpage, www.homewiththekids.com/scams/assembly.php .

Later, I will tell you how you can assemble products at home and make money. This, however, would be something you would do completely on your own.

CHECK CASHING SCAMS

Several check cashing scams exist. Most follow the pattern of what is called the Nigerian check cashing scam. It is named the Nigerian check cashing scam, because it seems this fraud originated from Nigeria. The scam runs as follows.

Usually, the victim is contacted by email or even possibly through Facebook, although he may be contacted by letter or fax. The perpetrator says in a message they need to transfer money internationally, but have run into some sort of roadblock when they tried to complete the transaction themselves. The reason is stated as being to avoid taxes, corrupt government officials trying to receive a portion of the transfer amount, etc. Facebook will take away privileges for those caught running scams there, it should be noted.

The perpetrator is offering the victim a percentage or commission for helping to complete the transaction.   The perpetrator offers official-looking contracts, letters, etc., to convince the victim this endeavor is real. Once the victim promises his cooperation, the perpetrator sends a bank draft (or occasionally a wire transfer to the victim's account).

Once the victim deposits the draft, they can check to see that the money is deposited there. They always find it is. They then are to issue a check or wire transfer to the perpetrator for the amount of the draft minus their fee for helping in the transfer. All seems fine.

However, up to a few weeks later, the victim's bank tells them the draft was not covered and the victim has to make up the amount they sent to the perpetrator, plus the amount they kept for their fee. Since the transfer was usually for thousands of dollars, the victim is out much money.

The victim wonders how a draft can clear and yet be no good. The reason is the bank deposits the draft with the condition that it will only be honored once it is cleared by the issuing institution. Since this always involves an overseas bank, the time to do this can be considerable. The credit union I use makes checking whether a draft has cleared an easy process. Online, all recent deposits are listed and if one has not yet cleared the website says as much.

In another twist on this, the perpetrator asks for the victim's account information, such as account number, PIN, etc., so the money can be wired to the account. If the victim gives out this information, the scammer possibly could withdraw all the money from the account. Never, ever give your account information to anyone about whom you have any doubts at all. To be perfectly safe, never give out any more information to any business contact than you are required to give.

In still another twist to this, the victim may be invited to the foreign country (usually Nigeria) to check out this scheme and to complete the transaction. The Florida attorney general's website says there are persons who have done this and were beaten, subjected to threats and extortion and even murdered.

Ask yourself these questions, if you are approached with this or a similar scheme:

- If, for some reason, you needed help to transfer money out of another country, would you look to a complete stranger for help? I hope not.
- Why would someone from another country look to you, a complete stranger, to help them transfer their money?

- Why would someone from another country offer to share their wealth with you, a complete stranger?
- If the opportunity is for real, what could be the consequences for me? A very small number of these offers could be for real. If they are, then they are illegal money-laundering schemes. Cases have been reported where persons became involved in these schemes and were actually paid as promised. However, the authorities came down on them, as these schemes were perpetrated to launder illegal drug money or other money that could not be legally handled. The victims ended up dealing with law enforcement authorities and sometimes had assets seized or had the threat of prosecution hanging over their heads. If you have to get an attorney to help you in such a situation, it can become very costly.
- Is there a risk to opening emails with these offers? Yes, there is. Instances have been recorded where opening these emails resulted in actions being set into motion against the victim's computer or data on the victim's computer. Sometimes people have sent such emails with the intention of disabling the receiving computer or erasing the hard drive. Also, programs have been downloaded with the email that enabled the sender to access information on the victim's computer. You never want someone you do not know accessing sensitive information from you. You do not know how it will be used. Always have a good security program on your computer. Such a program (Norton, Webroot, etc.) will in most cases warn you when encountering a suspect email, but hackers sometimes get around computer security.

Just look at headline news to see huge cases of data breaches.

For further details on the Nigerian money scheme, see the following, from which I used some of the information presented here:

- The pages about scams from the Maine Attorney general's website, www.maine.gov/ag/consumer/scams.shtml .
- The MSN career builder website, http://msn.careerbuilder.com .
- The Florida attorney general website, referenced a few paragraphs above.
- The BBC news website, http://news.bbc.co.uk .

There are other variations on the Nigerian money scam. I will show a couple examples that surfaced in my home area, Highlands County, Florida. The first was sent to a local church. Here is the gist of it, as told to the congregation by the church's pastor:

A South African lawyer faxed a letter addressed to the president of our church and offered a share in a twenty-five million dollar cash estate if he would claim to be the next of kin to the deceased man. The dead man had no relatives and the lawyer did not want the government to get the money.

Now this lawyer wants a church leader to claim to be the next of kin and believes that through his "honest" co-operation that he can get the money. His take in this scheme would be over ten million.

This whole thing stinks. This "lawyer" wants to get into someone's pocket or bank account. He's not going to hand millions of dollars in cash over to me or anyone else. But if I gave him my bank account number in order to send the money to me, he could then get into my account and steal what I have. That's what he really wants to do. [From the April 15, 2007, Bible Fellowship Church bulletin.]

Obviously this venture is a scam. Unfortunately, people let their greed and imaginations get in the way of their good judgment.

Here is the second example, which surfaced a few months later. It was sent to someone via email:

Dear sir/ma,

Please permit me to write you irrespective of the fact we have not met before. I got your contact through network online hence I decided to write you. I would be very interested in offering you a part-time paying job in which you could earn up to $4,000 a month in extra income. Getting an accountant in the USA/Canada or opening an account would have been my best choice if I was not working on a deadline that must meet a 24 hour turn around time, other options are on my side due to time, money, and requirements. This is why I am offering a pert time opportunity to someone responsible who can supply prompt assistant and service.

JOB DESCRIPTION:

Work as my payment assistant in charge of collecting and processing the payments from the associates.

1. Receive payment (inform of money orders/checks) from my Clients/Associates.
2. Cash the Payments at your Bank
3. Deduct 10%, which will be your percentage/pay on Payment processed.
4. You will then forward the balance via Western Union Money Transfer according to my instruction . . . .

IS THIS LEGAL? YES

It is very legal (article 15.3) Employment Opportunity Act. My lawyer checked all legal provisions concerning any domestic or international law against businesses or deals of domestic monetary trade. Doing this business is 100% safe and legal. I would be glad if you accept my proposal . . . .

Please reply via email with complete information
as requested:

NAME, ADDRESS . . . , PHONE NUMBER,
AGE,
SEX,
OCCUPATION
E MAIL

All replies should be sent to . . . .

Now, let's examine what is wrong with this situation. First,
I will tell you I copied the language exactly as it was sent
by email. If you will notice, there are numerous
misspellings and grammatical errors. Many times ads for
scams are not written with proper English. It's as if the
scammers are in a big hurry to post their ads. Sometimes
they come from countries where English is not used that
much.

Second, doesn't it seem strange that someone would ask a
total stranger for help in handling his money? Would you
go to a total stranger and offer to let them handle your
money?

Third, it seems funny that a business would want to use an
untrained person to handle their money. Why did this
person decide against using an accountant or established
accounting firm? That makes no sense. If large amounts
of money are to be processed, a business would want a
reliable, bonded firm to handle the processing.

Speaking of refraining from using an accountant, what competent attorney would recommend their client not use reliable, bonded accountants? Reference is made in the email about an attorney being involved in giving the email writer advice. This definitely sounds off key.

Fourth, it was a bad idea for the email recipient to have even opened this email. Something could have been embedded to do harm to the recipient's computer or could have allowed a hacker into the hard drive to access the recipient's personal information. I get a number of emails a month from persons promoting some scheme or another. When I see them in my inbox, I always put them unopened into my junk email box, if they do not get sent there by my email systems. You should do the same. If you get any email you about which you have concerns or even possible concerns, do not open it. I give thanks to Crystal Hicks for presenting me with this email example.

I received information about another "offer" while I was writing this book and decided to mention it here. Someone sent an email to a large number of persons. Someone opened this, printed it and gave me a copy. He said he had this one carefully scanned before opening it. Never open a questionable email, unless somehow you scan it and are absolutely certain it can do no harm to your computer. Anyway, here is the main part of the email, with bad grammar and all:

Hello
  I am Jerry Foster by name and the Payment Manager of Diamond Group Company. I need a

representative who can be working for my company as online book-keeper and get paid without affecting your present job? We make lost of supplies to some of our clients in the USA/CANADA for which I do come to USA/CANADA to receive payment and have it cashed after I supply them raw materials. Its always too expensive and stressful for me to come down and receive such payment twice in a month so I therefore decided to contact you. I am willing to pay you 10% for every payment received by you from our clients who makes payment through you. Please note,you don't have to be a book-keeper to apply for the job. . . .

The email then asks you to provide your name, address, cell phone number and occupation. It ends with, "Please Reply to this Email asap Thanks for going through this proposal letter and we are looking forward for your favorable response in working for the company so we can become a good big and better company in northern America."

Now, let us examine what is wrong with this offer. Please note that the problems with this example are similar to ones that were noted in previous examples:

- I copied this proposal exactly as it written in the email. Scam artists are notorious for presenting material with poor grammar, incorrect spelling, lack of spacing between periods and commas and the words following them and lack of periods at the end of sentences. This example has all of this and more.

ASAP should be capitalized and not be presented in lower case, as it is in this example.
- Again, why would a total stranger come to you with a proposal to handle his money? You would not trust just anyone with your money and no legitimate proposal would trust anyone who was not bonded.
- On a similar note, please remember that a legitimate company would never want to recruit anyone other than an experienced bookkeeper or accountant to handle their money.
- Also, remember to do research into a company making an offer. I found three companies going by the name of "The Diamond Group," two in the USA and one in India. No company goes by the stated name of "Diamond Group Company." I looked into the company profiles for each of the three companies. This proposal is playing on the fact that there are two companies that do work in the USA and potentially deal with raw materials for manufacturing. Scams like to confuse people into thinking they represent legitimate organizations.
- I contacted each company to see whether they had a Mr. Jerry Foster working for them. One replied that they do not have anyone by that name working for them. I never heard from the other two.

RESHIPPING MERCHANDISE

Reshipping scams can get you into trouble with law enforcement authorities. A reshipping scam is similar to the Nigerian check cashing scam. This scam usually is brought to you in an email. There is no legitimate reason why someone would want you to reship packages for them.

At the moment, there is little activity concerning reshipping schemes. A few years ago there was much more activity concerning them. The activity died down as the USPS and the Federal Bureau of Investigation (FBI) provided the public with much information about them. Also, the FBI, with the help of the Nigerian government, conducted a successful operation to bring reshipping perpetrators to justice in 2004. This resulted in more people being aware of this scam. Therefore, its exposure made it more difficult for reshipping scammers to find uninformed persons to scam. However, this scam and it seems most others resurface from time to time once public awareness about them has dimmed over time.

The USPS and the FBI provide many details about reshipping schemes in which the perpetrators have you ship something. We will look at the information on the USPS website first.

One reshipping scheme, says the USPS, is where the perpetrators advertise on internet job sites offering contract work in merchandise shipping. It lists this ad placed by a reshipping scammer:

> **MAIL PACKAGES** from home without leaving your current job. Easy! Ship parcels from our clients. Get paid $24 per parcel. Info at our corporate website: . . . .

In this case someone purchased merchandise with stolen credit cards and needed someone to unknowingly send the merchandise out of the U.S. The return address labels provided to the scam victims contained invalid return addresses, so even if the packages were intercepted, they could not be traced back to the scammer.

Such schemes were more numerous before the FBI cracked down on them. Helping ship stolen goods is a felony. Also, you can be convicted of postal fraud for shipping stolen goods. Even if you unwittingly help with this, you can be prosecuted.

Another way reshipping scammers operate is by posting phony information on dating websites. Since dating websites are quite common, scammers have decided to misuse these sites. Photos and fake personal information has been posted on these websites to attract persons looking for someone to date online.

Once the scammers befriend someone, they give them a hard luck story about hardships in Nigeria or other foreign countries, sometimes in Europe. The scammer tells the person they have netted that is it hard to get packages into these areas and ask for the person to help send the packages for them. Sometimes, the scammer tells the person the merchandise sent is donated for charity to help the poor. Again, in reality, the merchandise has been purchased with stolen credit cards.

The USPS and FBI Supervisory Agent Dale Miskell describe how these fake postings work (for complete information, please see the USPS website, the FBI website [www.fbi.gov] and the Computer Crime Research Center website [www.crime-research.org/news/]).

Let us look at an FBI operation that resulted in a major series of arrests in a number of reshipping scams that were operating from Nigeria. Starting in 2002 or 2003, the Computer Crime Research Center, the Merchant Risk Council, the USPS and the FBI, through Miskell, began looking into the reshipping scams with Nigerian connections.

The FBI, the Crime Complaint Center and the National White Collar Crime Center were fielding 19,000 complaints a month concerning spam, phishing and reshipping scams.

Miskell and others from his group went to Nigeria twice to coordinate law enforcement efforts against Nigerian reshipping scammers. The Nigerian government did its part by putting together the Economic and Financial Crimes Commission (EFCC), a team of police officers and attorneys.

Miskell visited Nigeria a third time in December 2003. He stayed through the spring to help the EFCC make arrests to put reshipping scammers out of business. Miskell spent his days with several local officers from the EFCC. They began their days opening suspect packages that arrived in Nigeria for delivery. Many packages would be shipped in the box of one shipper, say UPS, and inside would be another box that had been delivered by, say Fed Ex, to an address in the U.S. Such packages within packages pointed to a reshipping scam, because adding complexity makes it more difficult to trace where a package is first shipped.

The next action took place when Miskell and two plainclothes detectives drove to the address where the package was to be delivered. They were to serve as backup for a third detective. The third detective, disguised as a shipping company employee, delivered the package. As soon as the person accepted the package the disguised detective arrested this person. Sometimes violence erupted, as crowds of up to fifty people milled around the scene, wondering what was happening and getting into altercations with the arresting officers. Seventeen arrests were made this way and $1 million of illegally purchased goods were recovered. This operation put a major dent into the work of reshipping scammers.

The Home with the Kids website has an article about reshipping scams. It adds a bit of information on reshipping scams not yet covered. Home with the Kids says a person who unwittingly ships stolen merchandise is termed a "mule." This article states clearly why a reshipping scam needs "mules." "Many merchants are too wary and will not ship packages to the countries the criminals live in. So they need your average appearing address to appear legitimate."

MEDICAL BILLING

Another scam revolves around medical billing. There are ads claiming medical billing is a wide open field. These ads always ask for an initial investment, ranging from $200.00 to $9,500.00. There are several reasons why it is very difficult to start a medical billing business from home. These include:

- The medical billing industry has fierce competition. It revolves around several large, well-established companies. Because the industry is monopolized by a few companies, persons who purchase medical billing software usually find it difficult to build enough of a clientele to recoup their initial investment, much less make a profit. However, if someone does have an inside track on an opportunity, this hurdle can be cleared. There are other hurdles, however. Read on.

- The home medical billing marketing scene is filled with scams. Many companies have some elements of scams to them, although most actually provide you with a usable product. Many companies tell you it is easy to make a living while putting forth little or no effort. Also, a number of companies exaggerate or completely fabricate claims that they can recruit physicians, dentists, chiropractors, etc., to help get you started, once you buy their billing package. Additionally, many lie when they say they have an easy to negotiate refund policy. In reality, many have little or no intention of returning any or all of your investment.

- There are complex laws, Medicare and Medicaid regulations and state insurance regulations to negotiate when you begin any medical billing procedure. The start of Obamacare initiatives added more complexity to medical billing.

- Patient privacy has become a very large issue in healthcare. Anyone wanting to enter medical billing simply must become acquainted with laws concerning patient privacy. HIPAA (Health Insurance Portability and Accountability Act) privacy mandates must be followed.

- Similarly, governmental and private insurance organizations many times set forth detailed and complicated procedures you must follow 100% correctly if you hope to have medical bills paid. We once looked into setting up a part of our business to perform home sleep studies. We simply could not figure out how we were supposed to do anything concerning billing. We could not figure out insurance rules and governmental insurance rules. We found the whole idea of home sleep studies hopelessly complicated and gave up on the idea. This is the sort of problem you will find if you decide to start a medical billing business. Just ask the staff of any medical, dental or chiropractic practice what problems they encounter when they perform medical billing. They routinely run into obstacles. In fact, there are physicians who leave private practice partly because of billing issues. I should note that many insurance companies now prefer or mandate that home sleep studies be done in place of studies in which patients spend the night in sleep centers.

- Because of the complications with billing, you may need to spend considerable time training before you become ready to start a billing business.

Home with the Kids gives much advice on scams in medical billing, medical transcription and medical coding. It says there are three types of scams concerning these activities. Here is what Home with the Kids says in its website (www.homewiththekids.com/scams/medical.php):

> The first [scam] comes from schools that offer to teach you the skills you need to get started in this field. They promote salary levels that, yes, a few people do make, but most do not. . . .
>
> Many of the schools out there do not prepare you for working at home and employers know it! . . .
>
> The second standard scam is to sell you a "pre-packaged business" in medical billing. . . .
>
> [The scammer will] tell you that for a few thousand dollars they will train you and provide the software and technical support you'll need to get started.
>
> The final scam comes from so-called employers who offer on the job training. . . . They will tell you that you just need to pay a few hundred dollars for their software, then they will train you. Generally the problems [are] . . . :
>
> - The software is buggy and quite simply will not work.

- The software works, but you never
  manage to do well enough to get paid.

Stephanie Foster runs Home with the Kids and knows firsthand about the medical transcription business, having worked as a medical transciptionist for three years with Medquist, a legitimate transcription business.

Some of the information for the above discussion about medical billing scams comes from the Undress4Success website and from the http://msn.careerbuilder.com website.

Home with the Kids also offers advice to avoid scams in medical billing and medical transcription, which is the next topic I will tackle.

If you really want to start a medical billing business, you need to either find an employer willing to help train you or find legitimate training from an educational institution that provides such training. If you look into a training class or program, have someone who works with medical billing look at the class and give their opinion of it.

Once you get training, you will need to gain some experience working as a medical billing specialist for a physician or other medical entity. You will need to do this, so you can gain insight into many of the twists and turns involved in medical billing. Only then can you attempt to start your own medical billing business. And remember what was said at the beginning of this section on medical billing. Medical billing is a difficult field in which to launch your own business.

MEDICAL TRANSCRIPTION

There are also scams in medical transcription. You actually can make a living or extra income from home as a medical transcriptionist. Three-fourths of medical transcriptionists work from home. We will further discuss legitimate opportunities to be an independent medical transcriptionist later. This short section, however, concentrates on the scams involving the medical transcription field.

Beware, there are sites that promise the world, but deliver little. Some say all you need is the ability to type and you can make really good money from home. They want to sell you their medical transcription software. In their site, they tell you they are a member of their local chamber of commerce and may come up with other official-looking seals. They may in fact be real seals. Nothing stops a scam artist from putting a seal in their site and claiming they are approved by the seal's organization, even when they are not.

In such cases, always check with the seal's owner to see whether this group has even heard of the medical transcription software. Also, check with the attorney general for at least the state where the company is located.

Of course, companies that are scams offer little but trouble. Sometimes once you get the software, you find it does not work properly or you are told you need to buy an upgrade to do all you want. Sometimes that does not work properly, either.

If you seek a refund, you get the run around. Either you end up not able to get a refund at all or you are offered only a portion of your money back.

In short, thoroughly check out any company that sells medical transcription software. None of this even addresses the fact that you really need training to enter the transcription field.

To find good training programs, check with the Association for Healthcare Documentation Integrity (AHDI). This group has a list of programs they approve. There are probably other acceptable educational programs out there. Run any you are considering through the AHDI's website, www.ahdionline.org .

REAL ESTATE

On television, especially late at night, you occasionally see infomercials claiming you can buy real estate either with no money down or for just pennies on the dollar. You are told to just send your money, ranging anywhere from $13 to $220 and you will receive extensive information on CD that will tell you everything you need to know about doing what is advertised. The infomercials are chocked full of testimonials from persons who claim they have struck it rich.

Even Donald Trump was accused of running a scam when he offered his Trump University idea. This has turned out to become a problem for him, now that he is running for President in 2016. There is still controversy and litigation involved in this case. Some of Trump's customers claimed they were sold a scam, while others said they were pleased with Trump University. Sometimes it is unclear whether or not to call a sales pitch a scam, especially when some pitches, such as Trump's, were offered when the real estate market was past its peak performance.

A few years ago it was easier to buy real estate with no or little money down. The problem has always been once a property was bought, the monthly payments would start and somehow there had to be a cash flow to keep up the payments. If one could hold on to a series of properties for a period of time, he really could make serious money. Then the property market crashed. Those who put all or most of the money they had into real estate crashed with it. It seems that after years of languishing prices, real estate is making a comeback. After information is presented on three of the most popular real estate infomercial gurus, the ideas they present will be fully evaluated.

A few years ago there were three big companies involved in the television marketing. They were Carleton Sheets Real

Estate, Dean Graziosi and John Beck's Free & Clear Real Estate System. All three have been rated by the BBB. Carleton Sheets received a "B" rating, while John Beck received an unsatisfactory (F) rating. Remember that when a company receives an unsatisfactory rating from the BBB, the company really has unsolved customer service issues. There is information with the BBB for Dean Graziosi under Dean Enterprises, which even two years ago had an "F" rating, but today has an "A-" rating. There is at least one additional report in which he and his business practices are mentioned, however.

John Beck's company, listed by the BBB as Mentoring of America, LLC, has many problems. First, the BBB requested basic information about the company, but never received a response. This is one strike against its rating.

The BBB explains its rating of Mentoring of America in its website entry on it, as follows:

> Based on BBB files, this company has an **unsatisfactory record** with the BBB due to failure to respond to one or more complaints and or two or more otherwise **unresolved** complaints. However the business has **resolved** most complaints presented to the bureau.
>
> When considering complaint information, please take into account the company's size and volume of transactions, and understand that the nature of complaints and a firm's responses to them are

often more important than the number of complaints.

The BBB processed a total of 409 complaints about this company in the last 36 months, our standard reporting period . . . .

These complaints were closed as:

377 **Resolved**
7 **Unresolved**
25 **No Response**

The complaints concerned a number of issues, with 222 regarding refund or exchange issues. The other complaints regarded advertising issues, contract issues, billing or collection issues, sales practice issues, delivery issues, service issues, customer service issues, guarantee or warranty issues and product issues.

Furthermore, the BBB reported defendants Mentoring of America, John Beck Amazing Profits and Jeff Paul entered into an agreement with the Utah Division of Consumer Protection on January 10, 2007. In this agreement the defendants were required to pay a $25,000 fine. The defendants also were required to comply with customer cancellation laws. The defendants were required to clearly disclose in their sales presentations what services were to be provided to customers and who was to provide those services. Also, the defendants were required to work with the Division of Consumer Protection to resolve customer complaints.

The BBB pointed out that in 2012 the Federal Trade Commission won a court judgment against John Beck's infomercials promoting Beck's Free & Clear Real Estate System. The FTC website reports more on this, saying a U.S. District Court found Beck's claims to be false and Beck was instructed to make restitution to wronged consumers. The FTC website said this case involved FTC actions against two other real estate systems promoted by two other persons ("FTC Wins Court Judgment Against Massive Get-Rich-Quick Infomercial Scam," FTC website, at https://www.ftc.gov/news-events/press-releases/2012/05/ftc-wins-court-judgment-against-massive-get-rich-quick).

As can be seen through the BBB report on John Beck's business holdings and the FTC case, these holdings have serious flaws concerning consumer protection. In this instance, a considerably negative BBB report should discourage prospective customers from doing business with John Beck.

Dean Graziosi operates a website, www.deangraziosi.com , in which he sells several books, including his book *Be a Real Estate Millionaire*. He once had infomercials, as did Carlton Sheets and John Beck. Graziosi sells his books via Amazon. Online customer reviews on the Amazon website, www.amazon.com , provide some insight into Graziosi's books and marketing practices. Amazon has a rating system ranging from excellent (five star) to poor (one star).

Be a Real Estate Millionaire has thirty-five reviews, as follow:

- 5 star   16
- 4 star   6
- 3 star   2
- 2 star   2
- 1 star   9

The majority of reviews (22) are good to excellent, while 11 are substandard to poor. One four-star review, written by C. Li, says, "Good reading material for understanding real estate. It helps me to learn something I have never heard of before about real estate." This review adds, however, "I wish the author had addressed the taxes and closing costs associated with real estate transactions. I would imagine a lot of the real-life stories might not look as rosy as the author claimed."

One three-star review, written by K. Nunez, says of Graziosi's book:

> PROS:
> First, there are fundamental pieces of information in this book that is important. For instance, due diligence, that's a necessity.
>
> CONS:
> But the book itself doesn't offer anything specific . . . . If you are looking for a how to book, this is the wrong book for you. If you

want to "feel" good and "think" rich, then this would tickle your curiosity.

A two-star review, written by Susanna Hutcheson, points to some of the problems with following the advice of the infomercial real estate gurus:

> As a couple of other reviewers said, this is mostly a motivational book. There's certainly nothing wrong with that . . . .
>
> Here are a few things you'll see:
>
> "Instead of looking for properties to buy, fix, and quickly sell (flip) for a profit, I look for foreclosures and distressed properties that I can buy for a major discount, rent to pay expenses, and sell when the market goes back up. For example, . . . I purchased a . . . home in foreclosure for less than $60,000. I immediately refinanced the property for $192,000 and walked away with . . . well over $100,000 after all expenses were paid, and I still owned the property! Now I can rent this property to cover the mortgage and when the home market takes off again (and it will eventually), I'll be able to sell it for a profit or hold it through the next up cycle."
>
> OK, so what's wrong with that? . . . . I have a number of clients . . . who did just this. They're now in bankruptcy. And the current market

"does" matter, no matter what the author would have us believe . . . .

Be very careful in taking advice from this author, or any other. You can lose everything you have in real estate --- especially in today's market.

Some of the one-star reviews are also worth seeing. C. J. Montgomery says of the book:

I found the book to be mostly hype and a whole lot of bragging on Dean Graziosi. . . . I really cannot tell you much more about the book other than he "walks on water" in his own mind. . . .

I attempted to return some of the products and I have never been treated so rudely in my life!! It took 50 to 60 phone calls and the best I ever received was you have called the wrong department and when I finally reached the right one, all I received was being HUNG UP ON!

I . . . run my own business and I have never hung up on a customer, ever!

To be fair, this was the only review where a problem with returning products was mentioned.

A one-star review by E. Falken says:

Using real estate as ATMs is in great part what has brought on the 'credit crunch.' Advising people to do the same old thing that got us into this mess is just plain irresponsible. Advising people to do it in order to become "Real Estate Millionaires" in the face of [disastrous] woes ahead is almost criminal.

Another one-star review says, "This book is not the best book ever written about real estate. More or less it is an advertisement for his real estate course."

I would not call Dean Graziosi's books a scam, as you actually are getting a product for your money. However, it seems there is too little substance upon which someone can make an investment decision.

The BBB and other sources have some information concerning Graziosi. The BBB has a report for Dean Enterprises, which up to November 2013 had marketed Graziosi's seminars and other live events around the U.S through Insiders Financial, LLC. Graziosi said on November 15, 2013, he was ending his association with Insiders Financial. Prior to that time, the BBB had documented a number of customer service problems with Dean Enterprises. After that time, Dean Enterprises improved its rating from "F" to "A-." Another interesting fact was what a report from the Phoenix area BBB said, "BBB has not received a complaint against Dean Graziosi since October of 2013." (BBB website, at http://www.bbb.org/phoenix/business-reviews/business-opportunity-companies/dean-enterprises-in-scottsdale-az-97004871/ ; "Will 2014 Bring a New and Improved Dean Graziosi Brand?," February 10, 2014, at http://www.bbb.org/phoenix/news-events/news-releases/2014/02/will-2014-bring-a-new-and-improved-dean-graziosi-brand/ .)

Dean Graziosi now has a blog on *The Huffington Post* website. An examination of his writing there shows he is providing factual information that could be of use to persons wanting to sell property. (See as an example: Graziosi, "Pay Attention to the HOA Documents," *The Huffington Post*, September 24, 2015, at http://www.huffingtonpost.com/dean-graziosi/pay-attention-to-the-hoa-_b_8185082.html .)

Since 2013 much of Graziosi's marketing seems more straightforward. Also, he has donated much to charities. Since at least 2014 Graziosi has had on You Tube videos entitled "Weekly Wisdom." He talks about being successful, searching for deals to make money and at times he still promotes his same old books. Just look for Dean Graziosi on You Tube and see what you think. Has he made a genuine effort to change his business into one based on integrity? Probably. Anyway, if you look at what he is now saying, just look at it carefully.

I found locating information on Carleton Sheets more difficult than I did on John Beck and Dean Graziosi. I spent hours and hours in attempts to locate reviews from sources that were not trying to sell real estate scams to consumers. I also found no information from various state attorney general offices. It is amazing that the name "Carleton Sheets" is so well known and yet objective information on Sheets and his products is not abundant. I did find the BBB report, which to restate gave Carleton Sheets Real Estate a "B" rating.

However, Sheets is associated with two other entities: American Marketing Systems, Inc., and Legacy Learning, LLC. These two companies have BBB reports.

The report for American Marketing Systems is given an unsatisfactory rating. The BBB explains why it gave this rating:

> Based on BBB files, this company has an **unsatisfactory record** with the BBB due to a **pattern** of complaints and has failed to correct the underlying reason for the complaints.
>
> The majority of complaints allege difficulty returning products and/or obtaining credit.

For the standard thirty-six month reporting period, the BBB processed 197 complaints about American Marketing Systems. 177 complaints were resolved and 20 were administratively closed. The report further says that American Marketing Systems uses the www.carletonsheets.com website. Furthermore, two of the "doing business as" (DBA) names used by this company are "Carleton Sheets" and "PEI Carleton Sheets."

The other company, Legacy Learning, received no rating by the BBB. However, the BBB says in its report on Legacy Learning, "The BBB has requested basic information from this company but has not received a response."

In the report, the BBB says Legacy Learning was formed by Franklin Covey Company and American Marketing Systems. Furthermore, one of the DBA names used by Legacy Learning is "Carleton Sheets Real-Estate Coaching."

46 complaints were processed by the BBB. Forty-five were resolved and one was administratively closed.

The www.carletonsheets.com website claims you can get Carleton Sheets' real estate investing program free. I tried to find whether that is true, but it seems you have to sign up first to find what is being given free.

Also, the site emphasizes the possibility of being able to stop working at a regular job. In one part, the website says:

> Imagine:
>
> > ➢ Quitting your job!
> >
> > ➢ Luxury vacations for your family!
> >
> > ➢ Early retirement!
> >
> > ➢ Financial independence & control over your life!
>
> **Don't Put Off Your Dreams Any Longer!**

Act Now! Limited-Time Offer

Two Carleton Sheets books are reviewed in Amazon.com. One is *No Down Payment*. Two reviews exist, a five-star rating and a two-star rating. The excellent rating, by Joseph S. Maresca, says, "The thrust of the work is that the deals are out there; however, buyers must do the extensive property research in order to place a fair valuation on the available deal(s)."

The two-star rating, by Uri Gofman, says, "Although inspirational, this program does not offer much more than the very basic information."

Sheets' other book reviewed in Amazon, *World's Greatest Wealth Builder*, received twenty-four reviews. They were:

- 5 star   9
- 4 star   2
- 3 star   3
- 2 star   3
- 1 star   7

The numbers of reviews are heavy at the excellent and poor ends, but light in the middle. Let's look at some and see what they say. First, let's look at some five-star reviews. One review says:

> This book is an overview of Carleton['s] course but it also contains some good information and is very suitable for the newcomer to real estate. . .
> .

This book will not be enough to get [you] started in real estate investing. His course is far more complete. This book will get your interest. The course will make you wealthy.

Another five-star review says, "If you want to get a taste for his investment strategies and philosophies – buy the book. And if you like what you see, I recommend the course for anyone who wants to make more money!"

A third five-star review, submitted by Joseph S. Maresca, says:

This is an excellent book for anyone desiring to purchase a property as either a first home or a vacation home. The purchase of a property on "nothing down terms" requires a lot of very meticulous verification work. Carleton's book points out all of the opportunities and pitfalls.

One four-star review says, "I recommend this book to anyone looking to save a few bucks in buying real estate." Another, by David D. Liesch, says, "I would highly recommend you either read this book or order his course."

A three-star review, by Baron Berwyn, says:

You won't get a lot of secrets from this book. It gives an overview, and may give you the motivation to seek further education in the field, but [it's] not likely you'll be ready to start doing deals with just this book. You can find his complete course for not much more money on popular auction sites.

Another three-star review says:

> Mr. Sheets is right on the money. You really can become wealthy by investing in rental properties, but it does . . . take time and EFFORT! To be successful . . . you must take some risks . . . . You must have some money to start with, credit lines or whatever . . . .

One two-star review, by J. Daily, says, "Mainly filled with testimonials and trying to sell his other expensive products . . . ." Another two-star review says, "It had some adequate information on real estate investing, but was spoiled by continued attempts to sell his courses for more information."

A one-star review says, "Mr. Sheets doesn't even show you his way . . . unless you want to pay extra for one of his seminars. Utterly disappointing."

Another says, "A lot of complaints have been filed against Carleton Sheets' affiliate company American Marketing Systems, Inc. . . . ."

A third one-star review says:

> The entire book is an introduction to courses costing 10 times the price of the book. The book is pure and simply a commercial for the more expensive course. That being the case the book should have been free.

By just looking at this sampling of reviews, it is seen that opinions of Carleton Sheets cut across the range from excellent to completely unsatisfactory. Apparently, some persons see opportunities to use Sheets' books to invest in real estate. Others write off what he says as useless. One theme that is seen in many of the reviews on Amazon is that Sheets makes a strong push to buy his other products or attend his seminars to gain all the information needed to use his ideas. A book should tell you enough to understand how to use his system without investing more money in other products, that is, unless you feel you want more information. I do not suggest persons have to buy something else from me to use my book to make intelligent decisions. I think my book provides enough detail to steer you away from the rocks on your voyage to make money from home.

Dave Ramsey, in an April 25, 2005, posting in About.com wrote this about Carleton Sheets:

> The Carleton Sheets model of real estate investing breaks people and destroys them financially every year. They pay too much for the properties and can't get them to create a positive cash flow. Real estate people are notorious for misunderstanding cash flow. They think if the property rents for more than the payment amount due, it has positive cash flow – and those of us experienced in real estate investing know that's not true. There are vacancies, advertising costs, lawyer's fees,

eviction costs and a bunch of other expenses that affect your net cash flow.

The British Broadcasting System reports another type of real estate scam in its website, http://news.bbc.co.uk . This scam possibly is more relevant in the UK, but is something for which to watch out in the US, as well. Scammers involved in this fraud seek to bilk people out of money through bogus property investments.

The BBC reports this about property investment scams:

> Investors attend a free presentation, which aims to persuade them to hand over large amounts of money to enroll on a course promising to make them a successful property dealer.
>
> Schemes can involve the offer of buying yet-to-be built properties at a discount.
>
> Other variations include a buy-to-let scheme where companies offer to . . . renovate and manage properties, claiming good returns from rental income.
>
> The properties are generally near-derelict and the tenants non-existent.

The Guardian, one of the UK's most respected newspapers, had an online article about scams ("Scams," written by Sandra Haurant and posted February 1, 2005) that raised similar issues as did the BBC article. This article mentioned a scam where the scammer was selling a course for several thousand pounds that purported to teach people how to make a fortune in real estate. Next, "they try to make you buy cut-price properties that have yet to be built – and probably never will be." See www.guardian.co.uk/money/feb/01/netnotes.scamsandfraud .

An ad found in one of the US tabloids recently read, as follows:

JUST ONE DEAL CAN MAKE YOU RICH!

Without risking your own money!

- **Easy to Learn**
- **Very inexpensive**

The ad then listed a website, www.learncommercialrealestate.com . The website touts the idea of investing in commercial real estate, saying it is very easy to enter this field and make money. Again, it is said all you have to do to learn this is buy the guide provided. Remember what we have gone through before. This is another scheme that leads you to believe you can just buy the advertised product and strike it rich.

Since I first researched this ad and website, it has gone inactive. The website, if not claimed by its original owner, is being offered for sale on GoDaddy.com .

REBATE PROCESSING SCAMS

Once I received a mass-produced postcard telling me the following:

WE'VE BEEN TRYING TO REACH YOU

RE: IMMEDIATE OPPORTUNITY to work as Government Insurance Refund Processor

- Starting at up to $37,532 per year DOE
- Work from home / Flexible hours / No weekends
- Processing Government Insurance Refunds to homeowners
- Duties include: Receiving, Screening, and Processing FHA refund notices
- No experience necessary

Start Monday
Call . . . .

Most of the rebate processing scams are offered via email. All offers to show you how to make money processing rebates are scams. Again, just too much is offered to make these proposals even seem realistic.

Someone several years ago asked me whether another rebate processing program, Process at Home, was legitimate. I looked into it and immediately noticed things

I did not like. First, I looked at the website. In large, bold letters the first thing to catch my eye was, **"If You Have 60 Minutes A Day, Here's How 4,389 People Are Now Making Up To $255.00 A Day Or More, From The Comfort Of Their Own Home!"** Now, to make $225.00 a day from a home job does not seem unbelievable, but the part of working only an hour a day to make that amount of money does.

The next thing I saw was a banner rolling across the top listing some of the clients serviced by persons using this program. The list included Apple, Blockbuster Video and Hewlett Packard, to name a few. I contacted Blockbuster Video via email and was told they had never heard of a rebate program using the name given.

Under that banner was another one saying the program was seen in *The New York Times, Esquire, USA Today,* CNN Interactive, America Online, Forbes.com and Yahoo. This is possible, but only if this program was advertised there. I checked Forbes.com and found nothing about this product.

The next thing I saw was the comment, in bold lettering, **"Best Part: You can try it FREE for 3 whole months if you want!"** Upon further inspection in the website, I found you must first pay online $197.00 by debit card or credit card to get the product. It was said if you did not like the product, it could be returned within 30 days for your money back.

The final item I saw on the first page of the website was in a box, "**Sorry Folks,** This May Be Our Last Day! **Filling Fast!**" This is designed to make you think you may be missing out on a great opportunity, if you fail to act immediately. As I, and some of the other sources I have quoted, have said before, you should never make a quick decision to buy into something. Always think about your choices and do some research into a prospective company.

My next step was to look up the company offering this product. I went to the BBB website. Process at Home, with a California address, was rated "F." The BBB listed a variety of customer service problems with this company. In the 36-month review period 354 complaints were made to the BBB. Of these, almost half were not resolved in a way acceptable to the BBB. 105 of these were not addressed in any manner by the company.

Some customers complained the company did not clearly explain the details of the free trial offer to use the company's product or that unauthorized charges were made to their credit cards.

Two other business names were used by this company and they had BBB reports. One was Angel Stevens Process at Home. This business, under the same ownership but operating in Texas, was rated unsatisfactory, because of complaints. The majority of customers contacting the BBB complained the company had a 90-day money back guarantee that it did not honor. There were 59 complaints on file against this company. Of these, 31 were resolved in a manner not acceptable to the BBB. Fourteen were not addressed by the company at all.

A third business name used in connection with Process at Home, International Data Entry, had a BBB report. It was located in still another state, Ohio. One of the managers was the owner of the other two companies. This company was not rated by the BBB. However, what the BBB had to say about this company was unfavorable:

> We have recently received calls from consumers. . . . Consumers state that there is a fee of $197.00. The 800 . . . number listed on the company's website has been associated with several work at home opportunities. Some that have been the subject of complaints with the BBB system . . . .
>
> Our office has received several complaints from consumers that have sent the $197.00 fee and found the offer not to be as advertised. These consumers have been unable to get the company to return their fees and have filed complaints with our office. . . . At this time, most complaints have been closed as unpursuable as we can not locate this company.

The BBB processed 47 complaints for this listing. Two were resolved and 45 were unpursuable.

Eventually, Process at Home dropped out of sight, but other such systems pop up on an intermittent basis.

I know someone who tried using a rebate processing program. He gave up quickly. His job was to notify persons that they were eligible for a federal government refund. The refunds to be given to people were genuine. The ad he answered sold him a system that allowed him to look up refund data in government records. One problem was some persons already knew they were due refunds and had filled out the government forms to get them. These persons were completely closed, even sometimes hostile, to the idea of paying someone else a commission for telling them about the refunds. Other persons were unaware they were due a refund. They, too, were all unwilling to pay this person a fee for informing them of the refund due. This man made not one dime and was out a considerable sum of money for being shown how to process these government rebates.

Undress4Success says of rebate processing schemes:

> Emails offering a job where you work from home
> processing rebates are common. Some suggest
> you can make $15 for each one you process and
> they claim you can do ten or more an hour. Yeah,
> right. And if you haven't fallen for that line
> they offer you double your money back.

I found another listing, American Refund Services, when hunting down information on rebate processing. I looked at the BBB report on this company. It received an "F" rating. The BBB based this upon the three complaints brought before it in the 36-month period. The BBB received no answers on any of these complaints. Although there is still information on this company, it seems to have disappeared since I looked into its practices.

As I said before, very few people are willing to pay someone a fee for processing their rebates without their knowledge or permission. All one has to do to find whether they have an FHA rebate due is contact their mortgage company or the FHA itself. The FHA website and appropriate page is www.hud.gov/offices/hsg/comp/refunds/fhafact.cfm .

My advice is to stay away from all rebate processing offers. If there is a truly legitimate offer out there, I have not seen it.

SURVEY SCAMS

There are legitimate opportunities to take surveys for money. These will be reported to you later. However, scams concerning survey taking also exist.   These scams have several variations.

One variation is for a scammer to simply use the name of an existing legitimate survey organization. American Consumer Opinion, a legitimate survey business, has for at least five years had a warning posted on its website (www.acop.com/) about a scam using its name to confuse prospective contractors and bilk money from them. The warning reads:

A fraudulent Canadian company is using the American Consumer Opinion name to mail counterfeit checks for thousands of dollars, instructing you to deposit the check and then wire part of the money back to them. The company falsely claims the money you wire will go towards your training to become a mystery shopper. This is a criminal and illegal scam. Do not attempt to cash or deposit the check. Do not wire any money to anyone. Membership in American Consumer Opinion is always free.

The other common variation is for a website to offer surveys to you that are scams. You sometimes know they are scams, because they request a fee for signing up. A legitimate company never asks a fee for membership. One site I found that no longer exists, http://www.business-reviews.org/ , told you 97% of survey sites are scams. Next, it gave you information about three sites that would charge you fees ranging from $34.00 to $39.95 to sign up to take surveys. As I just said, never accept a survey offer that requests money to join. Legitimate companies always sign you up for free and pay you for taking their surveys. I could not find a location or telephone number for www.business-reviews.org. Incidentally, a company exists using a similar URL. The URL is http://business-reviews.org/ and the name is Business reviews news. This is a legitimate company that is not involved in surveys. I am sure Business reviews news has gone through some grief over the company using an almost identical website name.

Remember, a legitimate organization will always somewhere in their site provide an address and probably a telephone number. Many companies are now also on Facebook. If these are provided and you have any doubts about a survey business, do the following:

- Check with the state attorney general where the business says it is located.
- Try to find the local chamber of commerce in the locality where the address is located.
- Also, check to see what the BBB has on file for this company. Remember, if a report exists that is positive, you still do not know whether the business is legitimate or a scam. However, if the report is unsatisfactory, the business has serious business practice issues.

A final good bit of information is provided by Home with the Kids. An article in this organization's website offers this advice, "Most people will earn very little with online surveys, despite the claims." And, "Don't join any survey that requires you to pay to participate . . . ."

Home with the Kids offers a free list of legitimate survey companies. I will present more from this organization later, when I present real opportunities to make money from home businesses.

Something came to my attention three times in one month while I was writing this book and once six months later while I was editing it. It does not exactly fit into any category of scam, but it seems to fit best under the survey scam topic. Actually, it turned out not to be even a scam.

I received four emails concerning a big cash giveaway from Microsoft. The gist of the emails, all four almost identical, was that Microsoft was giving huge fees to persons taking part in an email test that was an effort to promote Internet Explorer. This particular "offer" periodically is resurrected back to life by someone and has been around for a number of years.

The best way to explain what the email offers is to present the email itself. I made no attempts to correct spelling and grammar errors:

THIS TOOK TWO PAGES OF THE TUESDAY USA TODAY - IT IS FOR REAL

To all of my friends, I do not usually forward messages,

But this is from my friend Pearlas Sandborn and she really is an attorney.

If she says that this will work - It will work. After all, What have you got to lose?

SORRY EVERYBODY.. JUST HAD TO TAKE THE CHANCE!!! I'm an attorney, And I know

the law. This thing is for real. Rest assured

AOL and Intel will follow through with their promises for
fear of facing a multimillion-dollar class action suit similar to the one filed by PepsiCo against Gen eral Electric not too long a go.

Dear Friends: Please do not take this for a junk letter.

Bill Gates s haring his fortune. If you ignore this, You will repent later .

Microsoft and AOL are now the largest Internet companies
and in an effort to make sure that Internet Explorer remains the most widely used program, Microsoft and AOL are running an e-mail beta test.

When you forward this e-mail to friends, Microsoft can and will track it (If you are a Microsoft Windows user) For a two weeks time period.

For every person that you forward this e-mail to, Microsoft will pay you $245.00 For every person that you sent it to that forwards it on, Microsoft will pay you $243.00 and for every third person that receives it, You will be paid $241.00. Within two weeks, Microsoft will contact you for your address and then send you a check.

Thought this was a scam myself, But two weeks after receiving this e-mail and for warding it on. Microsoft contacted me for my address and within days, I received a check for $24, 800.00 . You need to respond before the beta testing is over. If anyone can afford this, Bill gates is the man.

0A
It's all marketing expense to him. Please forward this to as many people as possible. You are bound to get at least $10, 000.00

We're not going to help them out with their e-mail beta test without getting a little something for our time.. My brother's girlfriend got in on this a few months ago. When I went to visit him for the Baylor/UT game, she showed me her check. It was for the sum of $4, 324.44 and was stamped 'Paid I n Full'.

I knew this was a scam once I read it. However, two persons asked me whether this was a real opportunity. I promised I would look into this for them, all the while knowing I smelled a rat. Once I was done, I sent the following email to them:

> I looked into the great giveaway thoroughly. My first impression was it was a scam, as not even Microsoft would give away hundreds and thousands of dollars just for forwarding an e-mail numerous times.

First, the idea of making so much money with so little effort seemed unreasonable.

Second, I tried to look up the USA Today story. I found absolutely nothing.

Third, I found a reference to Snopes.com. I checked out Snopes. They say this is a hoax that periodically resurfaces. It has been around in various forms since 1997. Snopes says this e-mail will cause no harm to the sender or recipient. However, it has been e-mailed so much that it ties up valuable internet resources.

As I said, I have received this e-mail several times in the last month. It even was posted in the AARC [American Association for Respiratory Care] Asthma Roundtable website. There, several persons were upset that such a thing was posted there, as the website is only to be used for discussions and questions relating to the treatment of asthma.

Fourth, I wanted to check the reliability of Snopes. Snopes is given a C rating by the Better Business Bureau. There is a good article about Snopes in Wikipedia. The Wikipedia article, "Snopes," says Snopes always thoroughly researches the topics the Snopes owners tackle. They always try to fully verify the reliability of sources and usually do not fail to do so.

The bottom line is that this is basically a harmless prank.

MYSTERY SHOPPING SCAMS

Legitimate opportunities to become a mystery shopper exist. We'll talk about these later. However, some terrible scams have led people astray, sometimes by stealing the use of the names of real mystery shopping businesses.

One mystery shopping company, Service Intelligence Experience Exchange, put a notice on its website warning prospective mystery shoppers about a site that borrowed use of their name. A message in the Service Intelligence website, www.experienceexchange.com , said an imposter company involved in a check cashing and money transfer operation was using the Experience Exchange name. The message said, "We do not conduct mystery shops involving cashing checks or money transfers." The message also said Service Intelligence "strongly believes that this entity is fraudulent, and is falsely using our legitimate business names to scam potential shoppers. The general public is advised not to deal with this entity in any form or manner."

The Mystery Shopping Providers Association (MSPA), of which Service Intelligence is a member, in April 2008 said even more about this scam in its website, www.mysteryshop.org . The MSPA is an association of legitimate mystery shopping businesses.

The website's notice about this scam said:

> The . . . MSPA . . . wants to warn consumers of a
> new version of a check cashing scam . . . .

Recently, consumers have received what appears to be a regular check from a legitimate mystery shopping company, but the check is actually forged.

Consumers receive a large-sum check, typically between $1,000 and $5,000. They are asked to evaluate the service at a variety of stores and wire a portion of the money back to the sender while also evaluating the wiring service. Consumers are told to keep a portion of the money as payment.

The name of a real company usually appears on the check as well as real account information. The forgery of the check is discovered a few days after it is deposited, and the consumer is held responsible for the entire amount of the check.

Remember what we said about check cashing and money transfer scams a few pages back?

An article about mystery shopping in Wikipedia (named appropriately "Mystery shopping") adds more confirmation to the idea of using a mystery shopping premise to commit a check cashing fraud:

There exists a scam that uses mystery shopping as a premise for fraud, where a person is sent a bad check with a request to deposit it into their bank account, wire a portion of the money

through a wire transfer company . . . and keep
the remainder as a mystery shopping fee. . . .
People who wire the "remainder" discover the
check is bad and lose the money they transfer
and the wire transfer fee in addition to the
total amount of the check, often leaving them in
debt to their banks.

The BBB of Chicago also warns about this mystery shopping
scam. The Chicago branch of the BBB says essentially the
same things as have just been stated above.

Home with the Kids has an article about mystery shopping
and mystery shopping scams. Home with the Kids mentions
another variation of mystery shopping scam:

The scams come in by offering lists of companies
that hire mystery shoppers but you have to pay
for them. These lists may not even provide the
names of real mystery shopping companies.

I did some research on the internet and found a number of
sites offering to sell you a list or offering to take you on
as a mystery shopper, providing you pay a fee.

SCAMS CONCERNING BECOMING A SELLER ON THE INTERNET

In the last few years we have seen a proliferation of ads
proclaiming you can strike it rich, or at least make a

handsome second income, from selling on the internet. While it is possible to make money selling items via the internet, most people who do so do not make vast sums of money. Later, we will provide some information about how to enter the world of internet, mainly eBay, selling.

There are at least two ways scams operate. First, there are internet marketing seminars. Home with the Kids says, "As with many opportunities, there are real seminars and there are scam seminars."

Home with the Kids says to first look at what the seminars offer. Home with the Kids says:

> Are they offering you the chance to be an internet business consultant? How to run a web mall? Neither of these is terribly promising.
>
> These seminars may charge you thousands of dollars, yet their goal is to sell you more of their products. Web malls . . . in most cases . . . are replicated over and over to the others who buy into them, so yours is not unique and scarcely of interest to either shoppers or the search engines. Such malls are very hard to market for most people.

Home with the Kids also says some try to get you to advertise via online yellow pages. Online yellow pages, according to Home with the Kids, buy you minimal amounts of traffic. For more information, refer to www.homewiththekids.com/scams/seminars.php .

Another way, the most common, is for online ads to offer you free, or almost free, CDs explaining how enter the world of internet selling. The truthfulness of what is said on most of these sites cannot be independently verified. They have no listing with the BBB. Sometimes they provide very little or even no contact information for someone just wanting to ask a few questions before they get the product.

Again, a clue that these may be frauds is what pops up first when you open their websites. I found an ad in one of the tabloids. It started out:

> **FREE Internet Work-At-Home Program!**
>
> Self-made millionaire revels next jackpot on the internet!
> Limited free programs available!
> **No gimmicks * No scams * No tricks * No MLM**

And, yes, I spelled "reveals" just as it appeared, "revels."

Next, I examined the website listed in the ad. It opened with, "**Earn $30K a Month Working 20-60 Minutes a Day**" and "How You Can Get Super Rich With My Internet Work at Home Program!"

This looks just like another of these get-rich-quick programs, which are always scams. Further down, I read that the CD from this source was free. Here is what was said, "**FREE** program offered November 25, 2008 only!"

November 25, 2008, was the day I first encountered this website. Therefore, this offer was to expire that day. The funny thing is, however, I kept checking back periodically for almost the next month. The website would say the program was only offered the day I went to the site. This meant the offer would never expire; it would be renewed each and every day. Obviously, this website was telling a lie.

The website information scrolled on and on. There was a letter from the company's owner. Neither the company nor the owner had an entry with the BBB. Further, the website said one could make money from a variety of online businesses, including running a virtual office, running an online travel business, offering customers internet domains to buy, running blogs for profit and by promoting other websites online.

Next, was a table showing the monthly earnings of persons who had taken the free CD that was offered in the website. It was claimed their incomes ranged from $30,502.26 to $94,275.29 per month.

Next, came the box I was to click to receive the free CD. When I clicked on the box, another box opened saying I needed to pay $8.95 for shipping and handling to receive the CD. I could pay (online, by telephone or by fax) by various credit cards, Pay Pal or debit card. Or, I could make special arrangements to pay by check, money order or by direct payment from my bank account. I never pursued this route further. I closed this box and was sent to the box with the offer again.

Following this box there appeared statements saying everyone who received the program since 2006 was working with it only 20 to 60 minutes a day.

Finally, the website ended with another box offering me the free CD.

I did some research about this company through the BBB website. The company name did not come up. However, the owner's name appeared in connection with a similar company that operated from the same business location. The BBB rated this company unsatisfactory, with one complaint brought to the BBB. This complaint went unanswered by the business. Also, while the business had a valid license with the Nevada Secretary of State, the BBB was unable to confirm that the business had a valid local license from the locality in which it operated.

Another company I found on the internet offered to scam the unwary by a potpourri of methods. The company I found had a website. When I first encountered the company's website, it appeared rather simple, with only one page and a popup that offered to give me a free audio, if I would provide my name and email address. I did not pursue this popup further. This website promoted making a fortune through eBay sales.

I did, however, examine the website. I mined it for all the information I could use to pursue the company through other sources. First, the website started with the usual things scammers like to do: impress upon you how you can make a fortune. The second line of the website read, "**Discover How** [the website owners' two names have been deleted] **Make Over $50,000 + Every Month On eBay . . . Part-time From Their Home . . . And How You Can Too.**"

The website had the "education specialist trained by eBay" logo on it. It also had an "eBay Powerseller" logo.

I next looked for a BBB report on this business. It had none and the owners' names were not connected to any other business with a report from the BBB.

I went to the eBay Education Specialist Directory, located at www.poweru.net/ebay/student/searchIndex.asp , to find information about these education specialists. The "education specialist trained by eBay" logo is only to be used by instructors passing eBay's training program.

I never found either person in the directory. I then emailed the Education Specialist Directory to ask whether these two persons were certified by eBay. I was told they were no longer part of the eBay Education Specialist program and had been asked to remove the education specialist logo from their website.

I was also informed the persons and company in question were located in Australia. That had never been mentioned in the website. In fact, there was no link to guide the user to any postal address or telephone number.

I did research into the "eBay Powerseller" logo, too. I found at that time there was no such designation. There were at least four books with "eBay Powerseller" as part of their titles, but I found nothing else. Now (five years after this promotion took place) there is an eBay Powerseller logo.

My enquiries brought change. The company's website was completely revamped. It no longer looked the same. The education specialist logo and the powerseller logo were dropped and a statement said this company was no longer associated with eBay. I emailed the Directory and informed it of this, although the people at the Directory probably already knew this.

This new website did provide more information about the pricing of its products. All prices were quoted in Australian dollars (AU). The options ranged from buying one e-book for AU $27.00 ($18.00 US) to buying a whole course that included manuals, DVDs and CDs for AU $3,995.00 ($2,717 US). Or, you could pay for two to attend a three-day seminar in Australia for AU $997.00 (travel and lodging not included) or you could join a group run by the company for AU $49.00 ($33.00 US) a month.

The new site included, as well, contact information in both Australia and the US.

Another site I examined (www.best10workathome.org) on the surface sounded okay. However, upon closer examination there were more questions than answers. First, I could find no independent information on the company or the owner. There was no BBB report for it.

Second, the site for this company said its mission was to review the ten best work-at-home programs being marketed. One of these was a software program that allowed the user to use the internet to make money. The review did not say what the program did or how you made money. You had to click on a button that still did not say much, other than you had to pay $49.95 to get the program. The page with the price also contained glowing testimonials. Most came from people who claimed they were making fortunes with the software. This page was full of bold type, exaggerated letter sizes and garish uses of color. It just screamed "scam, scam, scam."

Also, the "review" contained exaggerated statements that most certainly could not be true, such as, "This system has been responsible for creating numerous online millionaires and has allowed countless numbers of people the freedom to quit their day jobs."

And:

> I have personally been using the UCS system to earn money online, and I am earning between

$8,000 and $12,000 per month consistently with very little effort. My close friends and family all use UCS to earn money online and are doing very well also. Even my 76 year old mother in-law started using UCS recently and is earning $2400+ per month working only 30 to 40 minutes per day.

If you believe all this I really do know of some swamp land in Florida someone would be happy to sell to you! You would not even know it was swamp land until a heavy rain came along.

This same website recommended a number of other work-at-home software programs and a reviewer claimed on the website to be making decent amounts of money from them. This website at some point has disappeared after I researched it.

At the time I was writing this section on internet selling scams I happened upon part of an infomercial early one morning. The product sold was Jeff Paul's Shortcuts. What little I watched claimed Jeff Paul was an internet millionaire. It claimed Jeff Paul's Shortcuts, which was a CD priced at $39.95, contained more than 100 ways to make money via the internet.

Many persons were interviewed, some relating fantastic tales of their own rags to riches experiences. They all claimed to make much money from Jeff Paul's Shortcuts.

Of course, I started my research with BBB entries for the company. I found seven entries for "Jeff Paul Systems – Instant Profits Organization" and two for "Mustang Marketing." The seven entries for Jeff Paul Systems had unsatisfactory ratings and they were almost identical, as the BBB considered them different addresses for the same company. Three addresses were in California and four were in Illinois.

This company had seventeen complaints filed against it through the BBB for the standard 36-month period. The complaints regarded the following issues:

1	Contract issue
5	Billing or collection issues
2	Sales practice issues
1	Service issue
3	Customer service issues
1	Product issue
4	Refund or exchange issues

Of these complaints five were resolved. The company did not respond to seven complaints, two were not resolved in a manner acceptable to the BBB and three were listed as unpursuable.

In addition, mail to all seven addresses was returned to the BBB, marked by the Postal Service as "Returned To Sender – Forwarding Order Expired." Furthermore, the BBB requested basic information from the company and the company did not respond to this request.

This alone is enough to steer anyone away from doing business with this company. However, there is more. Jeff Paul is associated with another company, Mustang Marketing, operating from one of the California addresses. According to the BBB, mail could be delivered to this address, as well as another California address.

Mustang Marketing was given an "F" rating by the BBB. This was based upon the 60 complaints brought to the BBB's attention. The numbers for individual complaints were not broken down. However, only 3 complaints were resolved with Mustang providing the customer a full refund. 57 complaints went unanswered.

Here is what the BBB said in its report about Mustang Marketing:

> This company advertises a variety of business opportunity offers. The offers range in price from $39.95, up to thousands of dollars.

And:

> Most complainants allege difficulty cancelling and unauthorized [credit] or debit card charges. Complainants allege they purchase the company's wealth building offer for a one month period, however the company fails to acknowledge cancellation requests, and continues deducting monthly charges.

None of the news from the BBB report is good. As these companies say over and over in their infomercials, "But wait, there's more!" The Amazon.com website (www.amazon.com) originally contained two reviews of *The Inside Success Show*. This book, written by Randy Gilbert, is an ongoing interview of Jeff Paul. Both reviews are one-star reviews, the lowest of rankings.

The first review, submitted by E. Brown, says:

> Google "Jeff Paul". You will see countless complaints from people who have lost thousands. Many people have reported that they don't give money back (their promised money-back guarantee is useless).
>
> Outside of their wonderful [ads,] I haven't heard of anyone who has made any money on this.

The second review is no more positive:

> Discerning and intelligent listeners will quickly discover that Jeff Paul is a massive self-hype guy, self-promoting his "marketing genius" by constantly referring to his own supposed success – yet, you never hear details on how he actually did something. . . .
>
> I would not buy anything he offers until he starts producing concrete, organized, specific

information of the topics he blathers on and on about.

Finally, one must take note of government actions taken against Jeff Paul. Jeff Paul entered into an agreement in January 2007 with the Utah Division of Consumer Protection. For details, see the information earlier in this chapter concerning John Beck.

In July 2009 the FTC filed an action against Jeff Paul and five others in the US District Court for the Central District of California. The FTC charged these defendants with running fraudulent get-rich-quick schemes. The FTC said in its website (www.ftc.gov):

> The defendants allegedly made false and unsubstantiated claims about potential earnings for users of these systems. They used frequently aired infomercials to sell the systems for $39.95 and then contacted the purchasers via telemarketing to offer "personal coaching services," which cost several thousand dollars and purportedly would enhance their ability to earn money quickly and easily using the systems. In addition, all purchasers were signed up for continuity programs that cost an additional $39.95 per month, but which were not adequately disclosed to consumers.

In 2012 the FTC won a court judgment against Jeff Paul, among other get-rich-quick operators. *The Huffington*

Post said of this, "[F]ewer than 1 percent of consumers who purchased the system made any profit, according to the court findings."

The Huffington Post went on to say:

> But the scam didn't stop there. After purchasing the system, consumers were automatically -- and unknowingly -- enrolled in a "continuity program" that charged an additional $39.95 per month. By signing up buyers for the costly program without the consumer's consent, the companies violated the FTC Act and the Telemarketing Sales Rule. ("Get-Rich-Quick Scams: FTC Cracks Down On Companies That Defrauded 1 Million Customers," *Huffington Post* online, May 1, 2012, at http://www.huffingtonpost.com/2012/05/01/get-rich-quick-scams-ftc_n_1467767.html and "FTC Wins Court Judgment Against Massive Get-Rich-Quick Infomercial Scam," FTC website, at https://www.ftc.gov/news-events/press-releases/2012/05/ftc-wins-court-judgment-against-massive-get-rich-quick .)

Jeff Paul seemed to have gone inactive at the time of this FTC action or shortly thereafter. His business Facebook account still exists, but has seen no traffic for years. His websites have been inactivated. Amazon still had some of his stuff available, but nothing new seems to have been produced for several years. All I found was a DVD that a review comment shows was still being sold in 2014 and one of his websites, http://www.freetrafficbigprofits.com/ , may still be in use.

The real estate and internet pitches come and go. I do not really watch the infomercials, but they still exist on late-night TV. There are always new players, but they all seem to have the same get-rich-quick message.

FORECLOSURE SCAMS

Another trend I have noticed concerning real estate is the infomercial telling the home owner how he can get out of ever paying mortgage payments again. This book only deals with work-at-home businesses and jobs and work-at-home scams. Home loan scams and foreclosure help scams are not covered in this book.

However, use the same methods to evaluate loan and foreclosure help offers. See what you can find in BBB reports. Ask yourself whether the claims made seem realistic. Check with banks and real estate people you know and trust to get their opinions of these offers. Check with your state's attorney general to see what general information they can give you. Check what chambers of commerce have to say. But above all be careful. Take time to investigate claims made. Many persons have lost their homes, because they have been cheated in scams.

DATA ENTRY AND TYPING SCAMS

Data entry and typing scams are similar in nature, so they are grouped into the same category of scams here. First, working from home doing data entry or typing can be done for profit. That will be discussed when legitimate work-at-home opportunities are presented.

It seems most of the time data entry or typing scams are presented via email. These emails are sent to hundreds or maybe even thousands of persons at a time with the hope that a few persons (or many persons) will fall for the scam.

These scams always ask for money for the details on how to perform typing or data entry from home. They usually do not ask for much. They ask for $10.00 to $50.00; at least, that is what I have found. Sometimes, if you even get a response, they send you back a set of instructions telling you how to scam people just like the scammer got you! Other times, you get lists of companies that supposedly are looking for home data entry clerks or home typists. If you try to find information from these companies, you find the people from these companies have no such work or you even find the listed company has gone out of business or never even existed.

Also, you run into the same hype that other scammers use. Look at these examples of stuff that was sent to persons via email:

Typers Wanted, make $12,000 - $30,000/Month

And:

Start Making $250 - $2500+ per Day! Work At Home only 30 minutes per Day!

I tried to scale by size against normal text in emails to show just how large these emails show when they are opened. They are also in bold type. No one is making such grand sums of money typing or performing data entry.

Home with the Kids (www.homewiththekids.com/scams) has an article about typing and data entry scams. This website says some of what was just said by me. In addition, it says:

> It's really not that hard to spot the data entry scams.
>
> The first thing to look for is the fee to apply. . . . They're generally low to encourage the "It's only a little money, how much can it hurt?" reaction. Remember the standard rule of work at home jobs: They pay you. You don't pay them, except in very special circumstances. . . .
>
> Many of these jobs will tell you that they will pay $0.50 per name and address (sometimes email address) you type onto their form. . . . This is the kind of things computers are far better at than human typists. . . . They don't need to hire you to work for them.
>
> So what happens to the money you send in? This is pretty much just like the good old envelope stuffing scam. All you'll get back is instructions on how to run the same scam, getting people to

send you money so they can get started in data entry.

FREELANCE WRITING SCAMS

There are a number of freelance writing scams on the internet saying the same old line that if you subscribe to their product you can make a fortune. You can make a bit of money on the side by freelancing. If you become established, you may even make a tidy sum.

However, the scam ads claim you can easily make thousands of dollars a week by freelance writing. Undress4Success (http://undress4success.com) gives you the reality of what you can expect to earn:

> At $20 an article that means you'd have to write 8 a day (that's one per hour with no breaks), 7 days a week, to make just $1120 a week or $4849.60 a *month* never mind a week. So right off the bat you can tell something's whacky.

I've done freelance writing for many years. Much of it has really been free. I got paid nothing and expected nothing, other than the satisfaction of having written something. Most of what I wrote for money earned me very little. It takes time to cultivate publications and publishers that are willing to pay you good money for writing. In fact, it is more difficult to get something accepted by publishers than it was twenty years ago. Many authors find online inexpensive routes to self publish. Don't expect to start writing and suddenly become the next Ernest Hemingway. Even Hemingway, as is the case with most famous authors, started by earning almost nothing from his pen.

The website, wgb, at http://theworldsgreatestbook.com/self-publishing-scams-2/ , has tips for new authors looking at the self-publishing scene. Dave Bricker, the website owner, has an article there entitled "Self-Publishing Scams: Keep the 'Self' in Self-Publishing." This article has many tips on steering away from promoters who do not deliver as promised. A number of authors, including me, made comments appended to the article, that have useful ideas. Basically, Bricker advises:

- Research publishing options before your book is completely written.
- Work with various publishing professionals, but only ones you have contacted.
- Own the rights to your work. Don't let someone take the rights to your work.
- Run publishing expense numbers, so you will understand how to keep expenses in line and not pay more than you make from your published work.

ANTI-SCAM SITES

A number of websites exist that call themselves anti-scam sites. I have told you about most of the good sites already. I would not say, however, that there are no other good sites out there that combat against scams. **I'll list the good sites I found, for your easy reference**:

- Ripoff Report (www.ripoffreport.com) (Just be aware this site does not screen complaints well.)
- About.com (http://jobsearch.about.com/cs/workathomehelp/a/homescam.htm)
- United States Postal Service (www.usps.com/postalinspectors/wahscams.htm)
- National Consumers League Fraud Center (www.fraud.org/tips/internet/workathome.htm)
- Home with the Kids (www.homewiththekids.com/scams/)
- Home-Based Working Moms (www.hbwm.com/HomeBizCentral/scams.htm)
- Undress4Success (http://undress4success.com)
- Computer Crime Research Center (www.crime-research.org)
- Merchant Risk Council (www.merchantriskcouncil.org)
- Federal Bureau of Investigation (www.fbi.org)
- The Better Business Bureau (www.bbb.org)
- Truston (www.mytruston.com)
- Chambers of Commerce for cities and counties nationwide
- The various state departments of revenue or departments of state
- The various state attorney general offices – see the National Association of Attorneys General (

http://www.naag.org/naag/attorneys-general/whos-my-ag.php) for a list of all websites
- The Federal Trade Commission (www.ftc.gov)

Unfortunately, there are a number of anti-scam sites that only halfway tell you the truth. They inform you why a certain company or offer is a scam. They rant and rave about the evils of known scams. Next, they offer you one of their own scams.

Undress4Success has looked at many scams and sums it up best:

> More and more we're finding sites that scream "look out for scams" and they're scammers themselves. Such sites are loaded with assembly scams, and that should be a clue.
>
> If you go looking for a job and are asked to pay for it, *DON'T.*

One big anti-scam site I visited is Reviewopedia.com (www.reviewopedia.com). This site reviews programs that offer get-rich-quick schemes and tells you the evils of these sites. Reviewopedia is chocked full of reviews of such things as the Carleton Sheets and John Beck systems. It provides many details showing why such things are scams. When I first checked out Reviewopedia in 2009, this site provided other offers that were nothing more than get-rich-quick schemes. As of 2015 this site appears to offer only legitimate work-at-home opportunities. It appears since 2009 this company has become much more careful about what it offers to the public. Still check out anything you find of interest on Reviewopedia by checking reviewed companies online and see what you can find, considering its past.

Reviewopedia has a BBB report, but it provides no rating and little information.

Another site I examined in 2010 was Consumer Rated (www.consumer-rated.com/). This organization has a nice website. It asks for volunteers to provide reviews of products. The site says, "We are dedicated to finding quality products . . . for consumers."

Consumer Rated tells you of sites it considers scams. One is Reviewopedia. Another is BizScamAlert.com. Consumer Rated also tells you the Better Internet Bureau has certified it as a quality site. Consumer Rated provides favorable reviews of a number of work-at-home sites.

I did some research to get more information about Consumer Rated. First, I tried to get information from the Arizona Attorney General, since Consumer Rated operates from Arizona. The various state attorney general offices almost never give you any information about companies unless they have taken actions against these companies. When no information is provided, this should not be taken as a bad sign. Therefore, this route obtained me nothing.

Next, I looked up the BBB report for Consumer Rated. As of 2015 the BBB gave this company an "F" rating. A couple of things in the BBB report raised my suspicions. First, the BBB provided a telephone number but not a business address. The street address was listed by the BBB as unknown, although the organization was known to operate from Cave Creek, Arizona.

In 2009 Consumer Rated said it had been favorably rated by the Better Internet Bureau. The BBB report said that year of the Better Internet Bureau connection:

> This company advertises on their website that they are "certified by the Better Internet Bureau." In NO WAY is the Better Business Bureau affiliated with the Better Internet Bureau.

The Better Internet Bureau, which lists its location as of 2015 in Kannapolis, North Carolina, is no longer even listed in the BBB. I decided to follow the trail to the Better Internet Bureau in 2010. The BBB had a report for it under two names: the Better Internet Bureau and the Better Internet Bureau Association. When I originally looked at the BBB report on this organization the BBB report gave it an unsatisfactory rating. The Better Internet Bureau Association has an address in Surrey, British Columbia.   However, when the BBB sent mail to the address, it was returned by the Post Office.

One thing that really affected this company's rating was best explained by the BBB, "This company has an **unsatisfactory record** with the BBB due to its failure to discontinue the use of the BBB's federally registered trademark when demands have been made to do so."

At the time I thought, "How can you trust an organization that steals the use of another company's registered trademark?"

Later, the BBB modified its report on the Better Internet Bureau. It changed its rating from "unsatisfactory" to "no rating." What changed? Well, first the BBB still said the mail sent to the Better Internet Bureau was returned as undeliverable.

There were two changes, however. First, the BBB said "This business has no rating because it appears to be out of business." Now this statement was false. The Better Internet Bureau website (www.better-internet-bureau.org) was as of January 2009 still active. In fact, the organization was trying to sell a program called the "BIB $200.00 A Day Club." This club is a special program that is to show the first 77 persons to sign up how to make $200.00 a day from the internet. As of 2015 the Better Internet Bureau is still pushing its BIB $200.00 A Day Club.

Second, this organization discontinued to make use of the BBB trademark. The Better Internet Bureau website in 2010 said, "The Better Internet Bureau is not affiliated with any local, national, or international **BETTER BUSINESS BUREAU** also known as the **BBB**."

I would like to display the Better Internet Bureau seal. However, the Better Internet Bureau does not allow anyone to copy its seal without its permission. I doubt the organization would allow me to copy it when I am not providing a stellar review of it.

Now let's go back to Consumer Rated. Its website has links that direct you to a number of work-at-home offers. I checked on one of these in 2010, Free-Surveys.net (www.free-surveys.net). Free-Surveys.net had various offers for work-at-home opportunities. As of 2015, this website shows up on the internet, but it is inactive.

I followed up on two of these offers, one for Opinion Outpost and one for InboxDollars. A BBB report exists for Opinion Outpost, but this company has received no rating. Opinion Outpost had in 2010 been under the name of Western Wats Center. The BBB gave Western Wats Center an "F" rating. The company had 73 complaints filed against it through the BBB. The company failed in six instances to respond to complaints. Both of these companies have websites.

InboxDollars, as one reviewer wrote, should be called InboxPennies, because InfoboxDollars pays a few cents to fill out somewhat lengthy surveys. The BBB has no report for this company, but the BBB has a report on file for another name associated with this company, under the name of Cotterweb Enterprises, Inc. Cotterweb in 2010 had an unsatisfactory rating. As of 2015 it has an A+ rating and is a BBB Accredited Business, so not much can be determined about it.

Another anti-scam site I examined was SOHO Jobs (www.sohojobs.org). This company in 2010 had a large part of its website devoted to exposing scams.

This company is a strange case. The URL www.sohojobs.org no longer exists. There is a URL named www.sohojobs.com , which is the same company, located in Orlando, Florida. The website will not show anything unless you set up an account to use it. It has a Facebook page that has not been active since 2012. It also has a LinkedIn page that has been inactive for some time. Both the LinkedIn and Facebook pages list the first URL. The BBB has a report for SOHO Jobs and lists it under the first URL and as existing in Sebastian, Florida. SOHO Jobs has a terrible reputation with the BBB, receiving an "F" rating. The BBB based this report on two factors:

- The BBB could not obtain much background information on this business. The BBB could not determine when the business started. It did have a street address and telephone number, but the BBB could not obtain the name of its owner or manager.
- Seven complaints were filed against SOHO for the BBB's 36-month reporting period. SOHO failed to respond to **any** of these complaints.

I hope these presentations on anti-scam websites are enough to help you conduct your own research when examining such sites. Beware! Some sites are very slick. Sometimes it takes much effort to determine whether a site is honest or it is a fraud. I found one site I will not mention, but I suspect it is a scam. I could find so little information anywhere about it, that I hesitate to trust it. I tried the BBB and they have no information. The site operates out of Carson City, Nevada. The local chamber of commerce was no help, as they had no information about it. I contacted the Nevada Attorney General and that office could not provide any information. State attorneys general apparently have no jurisdiction over websites, if the business conducts no sales from their physical locations but only from their websites.   This business happened to be down the street from the Nevada Attorney General's offices.

If you find a site for which only sketchy details exist, my advice is to avoid it. It is best to assume a site is bad if you can find almost nothing about it from any other source.

PHISHING

Any work-at-home scam may in reality be a phishing operation. Phishing is a term used for any attempt to steal personal or account information online. This is identity theft. Many times phishing is conducted by email. The scammer comes up with some sort of convincing story as to why you need to send him personal or account information.

Other times, people fall victim to phishing when they decide to buy into a promotion that in reality offers nothing. They provide enough personal data, so that their data can be mined and they can lose much money or have someone buying things elsewhere with their identities.

Many sources warn against giving out information. If you have any reason to distrust an offer or request, please check out the offer or request. For more information on phishing and identity theft, these sources may be of help:

- Undress4Success (http://undress4success.com).
- CarreerBuilder.com (http://msn.careerbuilder.com/custom/msn/careeradvice/).
- The USPS (www.usps.com/postalinspectors/wahscams.htm).
- Home-Based Working Moms (www.hbwm.com/HomeBizCentral/scams.htm).

REAL WORK-AT-HOME OPPORTUNITIES

"Do not let any unwholesome talk come out of your mouths, but only what is helpful in building others up according to their needs, that it may benefit those who listen." *Ephesians 4:29 (NIV).*

MAIL PROCESSING FRANCHISES

At the beginning of this book, I explained how you can make money processing mail. Please refer to that section. I will not be adding anything else on the subject here.

MYSTERY SHOPPING/CUSTOMER SERVICE CONSULTING

I talked about mystery shopping scams earlier. However, there are genuine opportunities to work as a mystery shopper or even do a bit of customer service consulting, which is a bit more involved than mystery shopping. Usually, to do consulting, you must first gain experience and education in customer service. Mystery shopping can provide some useful experience.

First, I will quote from several sources concerning mystery shopping. Second, I will give you some information based upon my own experiences.

Wikipedia has an article about mystery shopping. In it, Wikipedia says:

> Mystery shopping began in the 1940s as a way to measure employee integrity. Tools used for mystery shopping assessments range from simple questionnaires to complete audio and video recordings. Many mystery shopping companies are completely administered through the Internet, allowing potential mystery shoppers to use the Internet to register for participation, find mystery shopping jobs and receive payment.
>
> The most common venues where mystery shopping is used are retail stores, car dealerships, apartments and health clubs, as well as health care facilities. In the UK, mystery shopping is increasingly used to provide feedback on customer services provided by local authorities and other non-profit organizations, such as housing associations and churches. [From "Mystery shopping," http://en.wikipedia.org/wiki/Mystery_Shopping . Please refer to this article for more information.]

Home with the Kids (www.homewiththekids.com/scams/mystery-shopping.php) has quite a bit to say about mystery shopping. Not only does this company tell you how to sniff out fraud, but it tells you about real opportunities:

> [T]here are legitimate mystery shopping opportunities out there. . . . Pay isn't great for a lot of them – often $10 or more plus the cost of whatever they require you to purchase. Keep in mind that pay is often given at the end of the month after you did the shop; that is, up to two months after you spent the money. Not exactly quick money here. Add in drive time and gas at today's rates, and the pay is nothing special at all.
>
> However, if you get good at it, you can get multiple assignments on the same day in a given area (through different companies if necessary), and cut down on your commute time and other costs. There are some fun shops out there to do.
>
> I have links to companies offering free listings of legitimate mystery shopping companies.

Indeed, Home with the Kids does tell you about honest mystery shopping jobs. Just enter the Home with the Kids website.

The Chicago chapter of the BBB offers this advice, "Visit the Mystery Shopping Providers Association (MSPA) website at www.mysteryshop.org for information on how to register to be a mystery shopper with a[n] MSPA-member company."

Now, as promised, I will give you my take on mystery shopping, largely based upon my own experiences.

First, the idea of consulting the MSPA concerning any mystery shopping offers is the single best piece of advice to follow.   The MSPA is a trade association that attempts to regulate the mystery shopping industry. Only legitimate mystery shopping companies are allowed membership in the MSPA.

This is the official MSPA logo. Only companies who are members of the MSPA are allowed to display this banner in their advertising. Always consult the MSPA website if you are unsure whether a company is an MSPA member.

The MSPA contains many member companies from literally all over the world. Once you enter the MSPA website, just enter the service area in which you are interested. Africa is the only significant area of the world without a service area.

I have worked with two companies: Service Intelligence Experience Exchange and Market Force. I have accepted many assignments from Service Intelligence, especially for one supermarket chain. I have also accepted assignments from some fast food shops and I considered taking assignments for other types of shops.

I finally stopped doing mystery shopping a few years ago. There were several reasons, none of which involved anything shady being done on the part the companies for which I shopped. I just found it was taking much time and not paying that much.

Liz Pulliam Weston, in an article posted on http://articles.moneycentral.msn.com/ ("The Basics: Real work-at-home jobs") in August 2007, said this about mystery shopping:

> [Mystery shopper Barb] Webb said she makes about $6,000 a year in cash, plus free goods and services worth $3,000 to $4,000.
>
> "I work it in with our schedule. I look at the week ahead and think, 'Where do we want to go? What do we want to do?'" she said. "If I need to buy clothes, I'll look to see if they need a mystery shopper."

Some Internet-based mystery-shopping services include:

<u>Corporate Research International Mystery Shops</u>

<u>Mystery Guest</u>

<u>Service Intelligence Experience Exchange</u>.

I have found typical free things include items from supermarkets and meals or meal items from fast-food restaurants.

To take shops in a retail chain, you must first read material on the assignment and pass a competency test. For some shops this test is easy, but for a few shops the test can be very complicated.

The pay is nothing to brag about. In fact, it many times is barely minimum wage or not even that when you factor in time spent reaching a shop and the gasoline used to get there and back. However, there is a way with some shops to boost your pay. If a deadline for accepting a shop is imminent or has even passed, many times the particular chain will authorize a bonus for accepting the shop. A number of times I have declined taking a shop, because I reasoned to take it would only be worthwhile if a bonus was offered. If the same assignment was available later with a bonus added, I then took the assignment I had declined to consider at a regular reimbursement.

Almost all shops have a certain time period when you are allowed to shop, such as during noon to 3 PM or from 4 PM to 7 PM. Some only allow shopping on a Saturday or Sunday or on a particular day of the workweek.

If a number of shops for a particular retailer are within your normal driving area, then sign up for the multiple assignments, as this helps on commute time and gasoline mileage.

With most mystery shopping companies, you must sign up for direct deposit. They want to send your earnings directly to your bank account, as this eliminates the postage and paper costs of mailing checks.

Another tip is to set up your own company. You usually can apply for a company name with your state department of revenue. Many cities and counties want you to somehow register with them when setting up a business. The good thing about this is that you can claim all legitimate business expenses when on mystery shopping assignments. Typical expenses are mileage and sometimes office supply expenses and sometimes meals. You can make a partial claim on your federal income tax on meals if you are shopping several shops and eat somewhere while you are in the process of traveling from one assignment to another.

You will never get rich or even make an income on which you can live while mystery shopping, but you can add a bit of extra income every month and get some products free of charge.

CLEANING SERVICES

Before 2008, we made a few extra dollars with cleaning services. When the general economic climate deteriorated, cleaning opportunities dried up and we never pursued residential cleaning once the economy improved. In Florida it is easier to do residential cleaning than it is to do commercial cleaning. Commercial cleaning here is more regulated, plus in Florida you need a sales tax license when conducting commercial cleaning. When engaged in commercial cleaning, it is not quite as easy to get commercial contracts unless you go through the bonding process and sometimes go through a bidding process.

For residential cleaning you just need to get registered as a business with the state, city and/or county where your business is headquartered. You can place ads in your local newspapers and local newsletters, sometimes for free.

If you do residential cleaning, you will want to set standards concerning what you will do and for how much. Set a realistic standard and stick to it. Don't feel pressured to take just any job if it does not pay well or requires you to work at times you really don't want to work or cannot work because of other commitments (such as having a regular job).

I currently know of no one who makes their entire living from cleaning service, although I do know someone who makes some money this way. You can make part-time income and it is possible to build up a clientele that would allow you to work full-time at cleaning.

Just remember, you must build a reliable reputation or most persons will not want to continue using your services. I know one person who built up a successful service enabling her to work full-time. Then she decided to take a two-month holiday. She hired two people to perform the cleaning while she was gone. They did such a poor job that she lost all her good contracts and never could recover. She struggled to get them back and get new ones. The damage had been done, however, and she finally closed her business and went to work in a hotel as a housekeeper, making much less there than she did when her business was at its peak.

Again, keep all bills for supplies you use and keep track of mileage. These are legitimate expenses and can (and should) be used against your earnings when filling out your income tax forms.

LAWN CARE

Lawn care, especially residential lawn care, is an endeavor similar to residential cleaning. To start small is easy. Just advertise a mowing service. However, if you wish to expand, you will need to buy expensive mowers and at least one trailer. You will also need somewhere to keep your mowers covered from the elements. And remember, lawn care is seasonal.

Just like cleaning, you will need to decide what types of jobs you will accept and you will need to determine a reasonable fee to charge. You can check around to see what others are charging. Also, remember that you will be outside when you do lawn care. Many times you will be outside in hot weather. If you don't like being in the sun and heat in the summer, then setting up a lawn care service is not for you.

A few years ago, the real estate market took a big dive and the housing market is still not rosy. For a few years many houses were in various degrees of foreclosure and many were unoccupied, indeed, virtually abandoned. This results in the water being turned off and in lawns becoming brown and dead. When houses get an abandoned look, they are easy targets for squatters and vandals. They are also so much harder to sell. The real estate market is better today, but foreclosed and abandoned houses are still common.

In some locations a specialized type of lawn service emerged. There is a special paint used to paint football fields prior to games and to paint the straw put into highway shoulders immediately after construction projects. This paint makes worn and barren areas look green and much more attractive.

Now, individuals are using the same paint to recolor dead lawns. These persons are hired by cities and realtors. A person spraying a lawn can charge from $100 to more than $1000, depending on the size of the area to be sprayed.

If this interests you, check with local realtors, municipal governments and banks. There may be an opportunity to make part-time, or in some areas full-time, income from this.

Most of the information about this new concept focuses on Nick Terlouw, who started the Greener Grass Company about 2009. Based in Stockton, CA, Terlouw said in a news report that he had done about ten paint jobs in his first six months of business. While this is not much, Terlouw said he expected his business to really take off, as the housing industry was in 2010 still seeing many foreclosures.

Nothing newer on Terlouw and his company seem to be on the internet than 2010 postings. He does have a LinkedIn account, but it is very brief and tells nothing about his company. Even typing "Greener Grass Co." or the like on a search line no longer pulls up anything new.

Terlouw said he used a 50-gallon insecticide sprayer, designed to spray orchard trees, to spray the green dye used on the lawns. He said the dye would last three to four months. The price he charged did not seem outrageous, considering what standard lawn care would cost each month. (Much of this information came from Christopher Solomon, "What crisis? Some businesses are booming," http://realestate.msn.com/ Feb. 11, 2009; Bruce Spence, "Upscale Curb Appeal Goes Green: Man Markets Spraying Business to Real Estate Agents, Property Managers," www.recordnet.com/apps/pbcs.dll .)

The idea of using paint to keep lawns green has had new life breathed into it. One company in Texas has recently started a service to paint lawns that are going brown, because of watering restrictions during the drought in some areas. Although to mix the paint requires water, it is less than watering a lawn. Some in California are reportedly looking into the same method to keep lawns looking green during drought conditions.

RESIDENTIAL PAINTING

I have known teachers and others who work for schools who do residential painting in their summers off. Again, you probably will spend much time in the heat and sun. This can provide extra income, but few persons want to paint houses, fences or outbuildings for a living. Painting is hard work.

HOME REPAIR WORK

Depending on where you are located and whether you have the required skills, you can make some income, or in some cases a living, doing home repairs. To do this, you will need to have at the least good carpentry skills, as it seems carpentry is the most common of home repairs. If you have skills in plumbing, that would be nice, as well. If you live in areas where there is a shortage of home construction workers, doing home repairs is much in demand. Of course, at present in most of the US the construction trades are not doing well, as home building has not recovered very well from the housing bust.

Depending on state laws and local regulations, you may need to follow strict licensing regulations to conduct home repairs. A friend of mine worked full-time for several years in home repairs. He had done much carpentry work prior to going into business for himself.

However, he found he was always underestimating how long jobs would take. He consistently underestimated the amount of work involved to complete a job. Therefore, if you decide to take on home repairs, try to become good at estimating the time a particular job takes. You do not want to be underpaid for the work you do.

MEDICAL TRANSCRIPTION

I told you about the medical transcription work scams earlier. There are, however, opportunities for the experienced medical transcriptionist to work at home.

If you already have experience with this type of work, you probably already have some training in it. Prospective clients want to be sure you have the expertise you need to do this work.

If you do not have the training and experience, you need to get it. Undress4Success says any school you consider should have the approval of the Association for Healthcare

Documentation Integrity (AHDI). The AHDI website is
www.ahdionline.org . The AHDI and the American Health
Information Management Association (AHIMA) have a
joint committee, the Approval Committee for Certificate
Programs (ACCP), which approves medical transcription
training programs. The AHIMA website is www.ahima.org .
Undress4Success says some schools claim approval from
organizations that the schools themselves have set up. My
research also turned up accreditation associations that
were phony, as I found they were set up by the particular
school they were approving or were very closely associated
with the particular school.

**The AHDI seal of approval. Only
AHDI-approved programs are allowed
to use this seal. Many do and almost
all tell you of their approval status in
their websites.**

Now, let's get back to AHDI and AHIMA. Both
organizations have lists of approved schools. The Andrews
School is a good approved school that offers distance
learning. Its website is www.andrewsschool.com .

Another approved school is CareerStep, which is also
basically an on-line training school. CareerStep also says it

offers programs through other schools. CareerStep's website is www.careerstep.com .

The above two schools are mentioned several places. The AHDI currently lists thirteen approved schools. However, its website tells you to closely examine even the schools with approval, as circumstances can change.

Another source of information is the Home with the Kids website (www.homwiththekids.com). The site manager and owner, Stephanie Foster, offers help. She says:

> If you are interested in medical transcription, take a look at my medical transcription section here on this site. I give free advice. I worked in the industry for three years from home.

I did look at her medical transcription section, located at www.homewiththekids.com/medical-transcription/ . This webpage offers much advice. First, Ms. Foster recommends anyone interested in obtaining the required training either take a solid online course or take a good course in a traditional college, community college or vocational school setting. She mentions the Andrews School, M-TEC and CareerStep as being highly reliable. She says anyone wanting to work from home in medical transcription should first gain two to three years experience being employed as a transcriptionist before going out on their own.

The Undress4Success website has a blog section at the end of its medical transcription scam alert (

http://undress4success.com/medical-transcription-scam-alert/). This section has many reader comments about readers and their knowledge and experiences concerning medical transcription training programs. Included are several responses to readers by Undress4Success's Tom Harnish.

Finally, there are other programs out there that provide useful training. One is the U.S. Career Institute (www.uscareerinstitute.edu). However, they do not have AHDI approval. Keep in mind, AHDI approval is the gold standard. Without that approval, it may be difficult to find someone willing to hire you.

I happen to know the U.S. Career Institute offers good course material, because eighteen years ago I was managing a computer repair shop. I used one of this school's certificate programs to provide training for a couple of our employees and I looked over the material they were sent. The U.S. Career Institute is accredited by the Distance Education Accrediting Commission (DEAC). DEAC, formerly called the Distance Education and Training Council (DETC), is a legitimate accrediting organization.

Only programs accredited by the DEAC are allowed to use this seal.

Again, be aware that since the U.S. Career Institute is not approved by AHDI, prospective employers may not consider a training certificate from that school as proof of valid training.

Any discussion of home-based medical transcription should mention the earnings potential. The Bureau of Labor Statistics (BLS) provides a great deal of data concerning medical transcription wages. Of course, wages vary from one state to another or even from one part of a state to another. The Bureau provides the following wage statistics that give you an idea of what to expect in wages:

Percentile	10%	25%	50%	75%	90%
			Median		
Hourly Wage	$10.68	$13.45	$15.02	$20.36	$23.70

From www.bls.gov/oes/current/oes319094.htm .

As this information shows, you will not become rich as a medical transcriptionist. However, if you run a medical transcription business from home, you can claim legitimate expenses, such as equipment, paper and mileage, on your federal income tax return. Please refer to the information I gave in the section concerning starting your own mail service business under the heading "INCOME AND SOCIAL SECURITY TAXES ON PROFITS."

DATA ENTRY/WORD PROCESSING/TYPISTS

I told you about the data entry scams earlier. There are real data entry, word processing and typist jobs out there, however. The BLS again provides data on earnings for these categories. I obtained and calculated the data presented below from www.bls.gov/oco/ocos155.htm#earnings . The statistics, from the BLS, are presented as annual salaries, so I have broken them down into hourly rates. For word processors and typists, please refer to this table:

Percentile	10%	50% Median	90%
Hourly Wage	$9.62	$14.15	$20.83

This table presents hourly wage data for data entry keyers:

Percentile	10%	50% Median	90%
Hourly Wage	$8.20	$11.87	$17.29

These two sets of figures only tell what, on average, persons employed in these occupations make. They do not tell what persons who either work at home for another company or who work at home as free lancers make.

The Home with the Kids website has some good information about opportunities. First, both they and I must emphasize that you will need solid data entry skills before you can be considered for data entry and medical transcription jobs. The faster you type, the more you earn. Accuracy is also paramount.

For some data entry jobs, you are required to take a test to prove you are fast and accurate enough to meet an employer's or client's standards. Some assignments require you to verify what you enter. Obviously, you will need a high-speed internet connection for many of these jobs, especially for assignments where you are too far away to drive to pick up and deliver work.

Home with the Kids is a good place to find data entry jobs. This link has a list of valid companies that contract out work or hire home data entry personnel:

www.homewiththekids.com/work-at-home/data-entry.php

PLACING GUM AND TRINKET MACHINES

About twenty years ago I knew a man in Topeka, Kansas, who started a gum and trinket machine business from his home. He bought a few machines and placed them in various locations. As he started to make money, he bought more machines and eventually placed about fifty machines around the city.

At the time I talked to him about this business. It was by no means easy to make money. He almost quit several times, as he encountered many obstacles.

First, he had to find locations where business owners or managers would allow him to place machines. Many rejected the idea of machines outright, as they claimed machines would bring additional rubbish to the area. They said those who bought gum and trinkets, usually minors, would discard what they did not want on the floor around the machines.

Some would allow machines on a trial basis or on a permanent basis and all charged this man, Kent, a rental fee. In some cases the fee was too high and Kent declined the offer.

After finding a location for a machine, Kent would have to check on the machine at least once a week and in some locations several times a week. This was to restock and to collect the money from the machine.

Kent said a number of times persons picked the locks to machines and stole the money, the product or both. He said because of stealing and vandalism, he had to give up on several locations.

Also, at some locations businesses closed and he had a difficult time collecting his machines there. Sometimes management or business owners changed and the new managers wanted the machines out. Either they did not want machines at all or the new individuals wanted to deal with another vendor.

Anyway, Kent ran his business for five or six years. He only made about $1,000.00 a year in profits and decided not to pursue this anymore.

I ran across a person who made money from gum machines in a different way. He said he made a little money by placing about ten machines in various locations. However, he was a coin collector. He examined the coins from his machines. Some he added to his collection. Others he sold for a profit. It was amazing to hear that he had found so many coins in his machines, including coins from Canada, Latin America, Europe and elsewhere. Many coins apparently will pass as pennies, dimes, nickels and quarters.

PAID SURVEYS

Certain companies pay for the completion of surveys, almost all of which are online. Usually, surveys do not pay well. You can spend anywhere from a few minutes to 45 minutes filling out a survey. Once in a while you might come across one that pays decently.

Remember, to participate in a survey, you must be in the particular demographic group to which the individual survey is targeted. Many times you will have to fill out screening surveys, sometimes which pay nothing, to qualify to fill out surveys that will pay you more to participate.

Sometimes you can become involved in an ongoing focus group, which will pay you several times for parts of the process.

Concerning pay, many times the survey company will ask you to provide account information, as they will make a direct deposit to your bank account. This is why you must be absolutely certain a survey company is legitimate. Many surveys pay in points, which can be redeemed for cash or merchandise once a set level of points is reached.

I have participated in surveys from two companies, American Consumer Opinion and National Family Opinion (NFO). American Consumer Opinion still pays by check. It also has a branch that deals in surveys for persons working in healthcare. The healthcare surveys tend to pay better. American Consumer Opinion's website is www.acop.com .

NFO, at www.mysurvey.com , pays in points. One point equals one cent. NFO registers you in drawings for points, as well. If you are very lucky, you could win 10,000 points (equivalent to $100.00). This site once would send products to be tested by the participant, but now mainly offers only online surveys.

Another company that is highly rated is Survey Savvy, at www.surveysavvy.com . Other than it is highly rated, I have limited knowledge about Survey Savvy.

Home with the Kids also has a bit of information about survey companies. Look at their website for more survey opportunities.

CREDIT CARD REBATES

Some credit cards offer rebate points when you use them. Discover is one. Some cards marketed to persons with businesses offer points. In the case of Discover, the points turn into cash rewards. Other companies offer points that can be redeemed as cash, merchandise or air travel miles.

While using a card that offers points cannot exactly be looked at as having a work-at-home business or job, these cards are a way to boost the income of any home business. Also, the IRS considers rebates as income, so rebates need to be reported as income.

HOBBIES

Sometimes you can turn a hobby into a business. If you really enjoy something and can see a way to make money at it, try it. Stories abound about people who turn crafts or coin collecting into ventures. Usually they do not make much money, but occasionally someone hits upon a good idea that really works for them.

For instance, when I lived in Topeka, Kansas, I had a neighbor a block away who liked to make furniture in his garage. He then thought maybe he could make a bit of extra money by selling some of his creations. His garage turned into a full-fledged workshop within a year. After another year or so he was able to quit his job and concentrate solely on making furniture and marketing most of it to area furniture stores.

That was not the end of the story. At some point he got a shop in Branson, Missouri, to start buying his furniture. Branson, which got its start in tourism from humble beginnings, blossomed into a major tourist mecca by the 1980s.

It was at this time that this man and his family started marketing their quality furniture in Branson. After about another year, they decided they would move to Branson, as so much of their business was done there. The reports I got in following years was that they had a very thriving furniture factory in Branson.

This is an example of how someone turned a hobby of making wood furniture in their garage into a large business. I know of someone who makes crosses and rosaries. After she made a few for friends, she found a number of persons wanted to order them from her. She also started placing them in a gift shop. She has since started a website marketing her creations. This was another hobby that has provided someone with a steady part-time income.

I could name other enterprises of which I have knowledge. Anyway, you get the point. If you make something or collect something, such as coins or baseball cards, maybe you should check out the opportunities that may await you. See whether you can find someone else either locally or on the internet who has made a successful go of turning a hobby into a home business. This leads directly into the next topic.

ASSEMBLING PRODUCTS AT HOME

I told you about the product assembly scams earlier. However, some persons do assemble products at home for money. Many times these ventures start as hobbies, as described above. Home with the Kids in two nice paragraphs in their website tells you what you need to do (and not do) to make this work:

> If you really love assembling items, just about the only way you're going to get paid to do so is to sell them yourself. You might be afraid of trying sales, but it may turn out that it isn't that hard after all. You can create whatever you like and sell them at craft fairs, online on your own website, eBay, or even try to get local stores to sell them for you. But don't bother with the ads offering you the chance to assemble crafts for someone else.

> There are very, VERY few legitimate assembly
> jobs out there. If there is any kind of fee,
> forget it! [From
> www.homewiththekids.com/scams.assembly.php .]

I will go so far as to say, I have NEVER seen an ad from anyone offering a legitimate home assembly job.

Again, I will give you an example of a husband and wife who made some money assembling and selling crafts. This couple went to flea markets and area craft shows. They did this for a number of years and finally gave it up as demands at work cut into their spare time.

To find information about craft shows and flea markets, just go to one or search for area shows and markets online and ask how you can sign up for a space. Everyone with a booth or space can get you the information you will need. If you decide to look into this, write down on paper what the costs of supplies and space rentals will be. You can then see whether you can make money on your craft this way. If not, look into selling via the online routes.

The information just presented on hobbies and assembling products at home leads directly into the next topic, internet sales.

INTERNET SALES

By now you probably realize the internet can be used to promote many types of home businesses. You can advertise what your business offers and you can run a sales business on the internet. Many persons use eBay to sell products. If you want to use eBay or some other place to sell products, do not believe all the ads out there that say you can get rich quick selling there. Only scams would promise that. Most persons who sell on eBay do not make fortunes and are not able to quit full-time jobs and support themselves in this way.

Unless you have a unique product or a unique way to market a product, you will find there is a lot of competition out there. Many businesses sell the same things in the same way. Probably most make a bit of extra income. However, I mentioned one person who sells handmade rosaries and uses an internet shopping website to promote her work. Another person once made miniature babies out of sugar and sold these on eBay.

To maximize your chances, you will need to get your hands on information that can help you build a business. A number of resources exist. Some will cost you money and others are free.

First, look for the free stuff. A series of free online modules on eBay can help you get started on eBay. The courses come under the title "eBay University Learning Center" and are located at http://pages.ebay.com/education/selling.html .

These modules go through the basics of eBay selling and take about two hours to complete. A variety of free online modules on eBay can help you learn to buy, sell, market items, photograph items to be sold, etc. If you are interested in using eBay to make a few extra bucks, by all means look into all this free stuff.

If you decide to use eBay, you may want or need more information. More information will cost, but it may be worth the investment. You can find this information through the eBay education specialist directory, found at www.poweru.net/ebay/searchIndex.asp . This site contains information about classes and about certified education specialists.

There is on eBay a designation called "education specialist trained by eBay." These education specialists have taken a special eBay training course and have passed a certification examination. Only eBay approved education specialists may use the education specialist logo in their advertising. The company upholds high standards its education specialists must meet. If not, they will lose the designation. I found a case where two specialists lost their designations, as the business they ran became a scam.

This is one of the official eBay
education specialist logos. Only
education specialists in good standing
with eBay are allowed to use the
education specialist logo in their ads.

The eBay education specialist website allows you to search
for approved education specialists. You can find ones in
your area. Also, some eBay education specialists who meet
certain criteria can become eBay certified business
consultants. The services of the business consultants and
education specialists are not free, but may well be worth
the investment of a bit of money, depending on what you
intend to sell on eBay.

PET CARE AND GROOMING

Specialized pet services can be run on a part-time basis
from your home. In some locations you may be able to
market a dog-walking service. Also, persons run services
to take care of the pets that must remain at home while

the owners go on vacation. Some people also groom pets, either part-time or full-time. Anytime you run a pet service, you should invest in good insurance. Taking care of pets comes with a risk and insurance can protect you.

HOUSE SITTING

A similar service to pet sitting is house sitting. Some persons will pay to have persons watch homes while they are on vacation. This type of business can be good in areas with many seasonal residents. In much of Florida, for instance, the retired "snowbirds" from up north only live in their Florida homes in the winter months.

BABYSITTING

Babysitting is not just for teenagers or for persons who run a day care from their homes. If you like to be with children and can watch them while parents want to shop or work, you may want to set up a specialized babysitting service.

TUTORING

Serving as a tutor or providing music lessons is another way to make a bit of extra income. If you have skills you can teach students, tutoring or providing music lessons can provide extra income. The same is true for providing sewing or craft-making lessons.

BEING A VIRTUAL ASSISTANT

The virtual assistant position is a fairly new concept. A virtual assistant is an administrative assistant that works from home for a client, rather than in an office. Many businesses have begun hiring or contracting for virtual assistants for several reasons. First, the business does not have to expand office space to have a virtual assistant working for it. Also, many businesses use virtual assistants as needed. This means the hours are more flexible, but sometimes rush jobs mean the virtual assistant will have to drop everything in his or her personal life at a moment's notice.

Unless you have secretarial skills already, you may need to complete an online virtual assistant training course to begin work in this field. The jobs pay $13.00 and up. This information was gathered from Joe Taylor, Jr., "Stop Pumping Gas: Ten Hot Home Office Jobs," September 16, 2008, http://education.yahoo.net/degrees/articles/featured_ten_hot_home_office_jobs.html and the Home with the Kids website.

For much more information and job leads in this field, visit the Home with the Kids website.

FREELANCE WRITING

Many persons try to make money doing freelance writing. I explained earlier that many writing scams exist. Also, you may do much freelance writing that is not part of a scam, but turns out to be really free, meaning you get no pay for it.

I have done much freelance writing and have been paid or made a profit from only a few things. I write many things with no intention of doing so for pay. I have written five books and basically broke even on those. I have written many articles and have only been paid for a few of them. I have written and edited many articles for Wikipedia and Wikivoyage; you do not write anything for Wikipedia or Wikivoyage with the expectation of getting paid for it.

If you want to be paid, first develop a clientele of organizations that know your work. If you are an expert in a particular field, this may help you find freelance writing opportunities in that field.

Also, look into writing articles, stories and reviews for magazines and newspapers. Just contact these sources and ask whether they would pay someone to write for them. Again, they may want to start you out working for free just to see whether you can produce something they can use. If they want free work, ask whether they will at least print your name in a by line underneath the article headline. This way it will be easier to market your writing skills, as people will see your name in print.

To get information about good freelance opportunities, you can buy *Undress for Success: The Naked Truth about Making Money from Home.* Also, the Home with the Kids website has a page with contact information for businesses looking for freelance writers.

Another way to make money as a freelance writer is to write a book. If you write an informative book about crafts, finance matters, etc., you will probably have an easier go of it. If you are good at writing fiction, history and the like, you will probably find the going much more difficult. Everyone thinks they can write marketable fiction, while only a very few succeed in making any money at all at it.

First, look to see whether you can find a publisher that will take your work and pay you a commission based on sales. If you cannot find one, which is likely no matter how good your work is, do not fret. You can self-publish. Anymore even established authors are finding the doors to traditional publishers are closed to them. A number of established authors have turned to self publishing.

If you decide to publish your book yourself, stay away from the vanity publishers. These publishers will print a quality book for you, but they charge quite a bit for this service. It will be difficult to make money if you have already shelled out loads of cash that you could have saved.

You can publish a book on your own and save all the money you would have paid a vanity publisher. When I wrote my first book, I used a regular publisher. He would not pay a regular commission, but we worked out a deal where he would publish my book and I would do some of the work involved in the printing process.

That was eighteen years ago. I broke even on that book. The next two books I published totally on my own. In those two cases I probably lost maybe $100.00 on each book when all was said and done. It is too early to tell whether I will make money on my fourth book, but odds are I will make something, although it will not be enough to enable me to write full-time.

Today, you can do all the copy work on your home computer. That is what I am doing with this book. Also, you can find a printer and work with them concerning what you want in a finished book. You may also in some cases produce a book using a comb binder. You can buy the comb hole punch and the combs and assemble your book on your own. What you want in a finished product all depends on what type of book you are writing. Unless you are writing to a very small audience this would not be the way to go.

During the last five years better ways to self publish have evolved. Amazon.com, for instance, developed CreateSpace. I published my last book using CreateSpace and I plan to use it to publish this one. I am not trying to steer potential authors to this website, but two author friends used CreateSpace and were very pleased. I was pleased with my last two books, as I could not have created a better product going totally on my own.

If you use this product, you will find a number of options. If you desire, you can pay to have editing and cover creation done. However, if you take the time you can create an entire book on your own. If you run into roadblocks, writer groups exist and many of their members have used CreateSpace or other systems to create books. LinkedIn has a number of writer groups and you can see what others have done and ask questions. Also, you will see posts about CreateSpace, as well as quite a number of other self publishing systems.

Once you get into a system, you will run into a number of tasks on creating a file that can be published. Many may seem foreign, but they can be learned. Just charge ahead and post of your progress in one of the writing groups in LinkedIn. Two groups I found useful are Books and Writers from Promocave.com and Nonfiction Authors Association – Writers Network.

If you self publish, you will also probably self market. This is a lot of work and it can be frustrating, but I have found it very interesting. You will need to write a press release to go to your local newspapers, radio stations and television stations. Most of these can be sent a press release online. Not all, but some of these, will be happy to interview you and then you can tell about your book. You may need to follow up with your release, as you may hear nothing otherwise. Also, if you have a contact with a newspaper, etc., use that person, as a contact can make the difference between getting publicity or not getting it.

Also, consider placing some ads in publications read by your intended audience.

REAL ESTATE/RENTALS

When the real estate market is good, especially the housing market, it is possible to make money. However, you need to be extremely careful. So many persons have gone bankrupt in the last few years. They flipped houses. This means they bought houses, business properties and empty lots at what was a low price. They then either held onto them a while or made improvements to them. They then sold them. If you ever do this, be aware that you may need to take out a large mortgage for houses and business properties. If something should go wrong, you will be in a bad situation.

I never tried this, as I could see the potential for disaster. Talk to a real estate professional you completely trust if you should decide to get into such ventures.

People do make money in the rental business. Then, again, there are people like me who had bad experiences and would not recommend it to anyone. In five years dealing with renters I lost $9,000.00. I did all the right things. First, I joined the local landlord association. These organizations have loads of information for landlords and can steer you around many potential problems. The association even provided me with a sample rental agreement, which I altered to fit my rental property and used.

Second, you should always use a screening service for potential renters. People can seem to be outstanding individuals and yet have the worst rent and credit histories you ever laid eyes upon. A screening service is well worth the money. However, I found some individuals are clever and can hide major problems from a screening service. I had an individual for whom everything checked out in a reasonable manner. I discovered down the road she had major issues with former employers who she did not list. Since she was only at these jobs a matter of days or weeks, they did not show up in her work history.

Anyway, as I said, I know persons who have rental property and never or rarely have encountered a major problem. Just be aware when you rent out property, you are always at risk for major amounts of damage to be done and it is difficult to get bad renters off a property.

CARPET CLEANING

If you should decide to enter carpet cleaning, be aware that in most cases you will be competing with much larger companies. I did some carpet cleaning for a few years and made a bit of money from it. I had developed a clientele who trusted what I told them.

Many of the larger carpet cleaners advertise deals that sound too good to be true. They offer to clean four rooms for $100.00, for instance. Sometimes they even offer to clean areas for free. Once a person hires them and they show up to do the work, these cleaners tell the client what they won't do for the advertised price. Usually they charge extra to remove spots, to move couches, beds, dressers and the like. Sometimes they tell you they only will go over an area once with their machine or they charge extra if a certain amount of cleaning solution is used. When all is said and done, the $100.00 offer turns into a $200.00 offer or even a $300.00 offer.

When you are competing against such firms, it is very difficult to charge a price that seems to compete. Potential clients tell you about the offers made by the larger companies and they usually will not listen to anything you have to say. They just compare dollar signs, thinking they are getting a bargain with the big companies. Many carpet-cleaning services use advertising strategies that border on being scams.

ACCOUNTING/BOOKKEEPING/TAX PREPARATION

A number of persons make extra money from home working as accountants, bookkeepers or tax preparers. To work as an accountant, you will probably need at least a bachelor accounting degree and being a Certified Public Accountant helps immensely. To become a CPA in most states these days you must have 150 college credit hours, according to the American Institute of Certified Public Accountants. This does not necessarily mean you would need a graduate degree, but such a degree or graduate hours in business or accounting would help. Some work experience will also help, since a CPA is expected to have a great deal of competence dealing with accounting issues. For a complete description of what the American Institute of Certified Public Accountants says you need, go to the section of their website dealing with requirements and expectations for CPA exam applicants, at http://www.aicpa.org/BECOMEACPA/LICENSURE/REQUIREMENTS/Pages/default.aspx .

Bookkeeping takes less education than accounting. You may be able to keep the books for small businesses. You will still need to have a decent educational or training program under your belt. A good two-year college program would be helpful. Again, you will need some experience.

Tax preparation may be done by accountants or bookkeepers. Also, individuals taking a tax preparer course, such as those offered by H & R Block or Jackson Hewitt can work as tax preparers. It is still recommended that they have some experience in this field. This can be gained by working one season as tax preparer for a tax service, such as H & R Block or Jackson Hewitt.

One disadvantage about being a tax preparer is the seasonal nature of the work. It can keep you extremely busy from late January through April. Then the business dies down to almost nothing the rest of the year. If you have a full-time job, you will have to limit the number of cases you take and just let a number of others drop by the wayside. CPAs, on the other hand, sometimes do tax accounting work, including the filing of income tax returns, all year long.

For more information about finding bookkeeping and accounting opportunities at home, please refer to the Home with the Kids website.

OTHER WORK AT HOME OPPORTUNITIES

Many other opportunities are out there. I will not attempt to explain all of these. However, you may want to examine them. The Home with the Kids website explains about a number of other opportunities. These include working as a paid blogger, working in education, performing transcription, working in insurance, being a researcher, working in various types of technical support and being a translator.

Another source for all sorts of ideas is StartupNation. The StartupNation website, www.startupnation.com , explains fully what this organization does. StartupNation says, "It's our belief that everyone can—*and should*—own a business, whether full-time or part-time. Our mission is to help you do just that!"

This site has many ideas and it tells about persons who have started home businesses doing all sorts of things. StartupNation definitely forces you to think outside the box. This organization also sells a book entitled *StartupNation: America's Leading Entrepreneurial Experts Reveal the Secrets to Building a Blockbuster Business*. This book is sold on Amazon.com and has twenty-one reviews there; eighteen are five-star reviews and three are four-star reviews.

CONCLUSION

I will summarize in this short section what has been presented in this book. First, the mail processing scam was covered. Next, legitimate ways to process mail were presented. Unfortunately, the cost of starting a mail processing service is prohibitive to most persons, as a large amount of startup money is needed to open a mail processing operation.

Next, a number of work-at-home scams were presented.

Finally, a number of legitimate opportunities to make money from a home business were presented.

The best way to avoid falling victim to work-at-home scams is to recognize what a scam looks like. So once again, common elements of a scam are here presented.

- If an advertisement or offer provides endorsements from other businesses, check out these businesses. Check the endorsing business with the regulatory authorities, the chambers of commerce, the Better Business Bureau, etc. Remember, a firm with a bogus offer will not hesitate to provide itself with endorsements from either nonexistent firms or other firms engaged in questionable activities. If the endorsing company is known to be legitimate, contact this company concerning its endorsement. Scammers will not think twice about providing phony endorsements from reputable companies.

- Remember to look back in the section about mail processing scams. You can attempt to find information about companies providing offers through many resource organizations. These include:
  - Local chambers of commerce (especially where the company is located). Just search online for the county or city you want to examine and then search for that jurisdiction's chamber of commerce.
  - The various state attorney general offices. To get a master list of all the attorney general websites, go to the National Association of Attorneys General (http://www.naag.org/naag/attorneys-general/whos-my-ag.php) .
  - The Better Business Bureau (www.bbb.org). However, remember the limitations of the BBB.
  - Registrations with state and local governmental authorities. Any reputable business will have information about it by at least some government agencies, such as its home state department of revenue or local city or county governments. Many cities and counties require all businesses within their boundaries to be registered.
  - Ripoff Report (www.ripoffreport.com). Again, remember Ripoff Report's limitations.

- About.com (http://jobsearch.about.com/cs/workathomehelp/a/homescam.htm).
- The United States Postal Service website (www.usps.com/).
- The National Consumers League Fraud Center website (www.fraud.org/tips/internet/workathome.htm).
- The Home with the Kids website (www.homewiththekids.com/scams/).
- The Home-Based Working Moms website (www.hbwm.com/HomeBizCentral/scams.htm).
- Undress4Success (http://undress4success.com).
- Computer Crime Research Center (www.crime-research.org).
- Merchant Risk Council (www.merchantriskcouncil.org).
- The Federal Bureau of Investigation (www.fbi.gov).
- Wikipedia (http://en.wikipedia.org/wiki/). Wikipedia has various articles concerning work-at-home schemes. It also has articles about specific companies providing work-at-home offers.
- The Federal Trade Commission (www.ftc.gov).
- Scott Larsen's website about Amway (www.amquix.info). It should be noted Larsen has provided much documentation on how Amway worked in the past; beyond then it appears little has been offered.
- Truston (www.mytruston.com).

- Snopes.com (www.snopes.com).

If an ad provides endorsements from professional associations, go through the steps detailed in the above point. A scammer is not above listing a real association as an endorsement. Also, scammers sometimes invent professional associations that have contact information. These associations are real entities, but are not legitimate themselves. They have been devised to provide the scammer with legitimacy it does not have.
- Once, it could be said more scams originated in certain parts of the U.S., in particular Florida. However, today scams seem to be located everywhere in the country. Some even hail from foreign countries. The use of the internet to conduct scams knows no state or national boundaries.
- Does the business promote a get rich quick scheme? Or does it make claims that sound too good to be true? If the claims sound too good to be true, they probably are.
- Do the ads of the promotion use exaggerated letter size, overuse of capitalization, garish colors, overuse of exclamation points?
- Do the ads stress urgency? Does an ad say this offer has to be acted upon immediately or it will expire forever? You should take time to evaluate any offer asking for money or a commitment of money.
- Does a business stress that when you join, your primary goal is to constantly recruit new persons to

be placed under you in a multi-level marketing scheme? Stay away from such offers. Remember what was said earlier in this book about pyramid schemes.

- Does the offer contain poor grammar? Some scam artists are notorious for writing ads with spelling errors, incorrect sentence structures, incorrect use of words, etc.

- Does an offer want to recruit just anyone to perform a professional task, such as accounting? If so, does the offer seem to want to recruit anyone without regard to whether they have any qualifications to perform the task? No legitimate business would recruit a complete novice for a job requiring experience and/or technical training.

It is my hope that this book has provided you enough information, so you will be able to look for genuine work-at-home opportunities and avoid scams. I wish you all the best in finding the right opportunity to make an extra income doing something that is of interest. Happy opportunity hunting!

www.ingramcontent.com/pod-product-compliance
Lightning Source LLC
Chambersburg PA
CBHW030942180526
45163CB00002B/671